PRAISE FOR
Bravehearts

"*Bravehearts* is a love story written by a woman who knows the desperate emptiness of loss and the aroma of a return to one's first love. Sharon Hersh has brilliantly excavated the humility of redemption and has handed us a book that is a pearl of great price. If your heart dreams of what it might be like to live in the fullness of God's love, then this labor of love is the gift you have been longing to read."

— DAN B. ALLENDER, PH.D.

best-selling author and president, Mars Hill Graduate School

"A book of inspiration, challenge, and courage. *Bravehearts* will take you to new levels in your understanding and experience of relationships. This is a must-read for every woman who wants to give and receive extravagant love."

— DENNIS AND BARBARA RAINEY

marriage and family authors, co-hosts FamilyLife Today *radio*

"Her true stories and personal transparency will dispel your fears and provide you with a pathway for making genuine friendships. You'll laugh, you'll cry, and you'll identify with Sharon as she shows you how to lay aside fear and experience extravagant love and genuine acceptance in your many relationships."

— SUSAN YATES

best-selling author

"From ten years' experience in singles ministry, the most common struggle I have seen in women is what to do with the continual disappointment of unmet longings. Where most run away from their true heart by denying or controlling these God-given desires, Sharon invites 'Bravehearts' into another path that can deliver true hope for the love we all crave. *Bravehearts* honors the hearts of all women like few books I have read!"

—REV. DAVID MESERVE

pastor of adult ministries, Cherry Hills Community Church, Highlands Ranch, CO

"Sharon Hersh explains a woman's need for—and innate skill in—expressing extravagant love. She not only gives me permission to ask for the relationship I want with my husband and friends but to expect that a large measure of what I want is also God's desire for me. Yet she doesn't leave us merely comfortable and content with validation. Rather she encourages and lures us with her own story and those of her clients and friends to engage intentionally in the hard work of loving."

—MARY JENSEN

author and conference speaker

BRAVE
HEARTS

SHARON
A. HERSH

BRAVE

UNLOCKING THE COURAGE *to* LOVE WITH ABANDON

HEARTS

WATERBROOK
PRESS

BRAVEHEARTS
PUBLISHED BY WATERBROOK PRESS
2375 Telstar Drive, Suite 160
Colorado Springs, Colorado 80920
A division of Random House, Inc.

All scripture quotations, unless otherwise indicated, are taken from the *Holy Bible, New International Version®*. NIV®. Copyright © 1973, 1978, 1984 by International Bible Society. Used by permission of Zondervan Publishing House. All rights reserved. Scripture quotations also taken from *The Message*. Copyright © by Eugene H. Peterson 1993, 1994, 1995. Used by permission of NavPress Publishing Group. Scripture quotations marked (NASB) are taken from the *New American Standard Bible®*. © Copyright The Lockman Foundation 1960, 1962, 1963, 1968, 1971, 1972, 1973, 1975, 1977, 1995. Used by permission. Scripture quotations marked (RSV) are taken from *The Revised Standard Version of the Bible,* copyright © 1946, 1952, and 1971 by the Division of Christian Education of the National Council of the Churches of Christ in the USA. Used by permission. Scripture quotations marked (KJV) are taken from the *King James Version.*

Details in some anecdotes and stories have been changed to protect the identities of the persons involved.

ISBN 1-57856-296-1

Library of Congress Cataloging-in-Publication Data
Hersh, Sharon A.
    Bravehearts : unlocking the courage to love with abandon / by Sharon A. Hersh.—1st ed.
        p.   cm.
    Includes bibliographical references.
    ISBN 1-57856-296-1
        1. Women—Religious life.   2. Interpersonal relations—Religious aspects—Christianity.
    I. Title: Bravehearts.   II. Title.
    BV4527 .H48 2000
    248.48'43—dc21   00-035943

Printed in the United States of America

2001

10 9 8 7 6 5 4

To my daughter, Kristin.
May your already brave heart become brighter and more beautiful
as God works in your life and you become like him.

Contents

Acknowledgments

My gratitude to my family—I hold you close in my heart every day of my life. To my children, Kristin and Graham, for your encouragement and gentle reminders that I still have a lot to learn! To my parents, John and Kathleen Baker, for your love and support. To my husband, Dave, not a day goes by that I do not learn from you about living and loving courageously.

To my friends who read and commented on this book as it evolved: Joan Shearer, Pam Pedrow, Judy Schindler, Lisa Lauffer. I can never repay the immeasurable debt I owe you for all your friendship has given me.

"Thank you" feels inadequate to express my heart to all of the brave women who have allowed me to participate in, to be transformed by, and to share your stories of courage and extravagant love. Thank you. My heart is full.

To Liz Heaney, I offer my gratitude for suggesting this book. To Water-Brook Press, thank you for publishing the words and stories of ordinary women who long to live extraordinary lives. And to my editor, Traci Mullins, your work is the most extravagant of all as it breathes form into ideas and gives shape to imagination. Working with you is a privilege.

PART I

THE HUNGRY HEART

CHAPTER 1

What Do You Live For?

"I'm sixty years old. I've lived over half of my life, and I'm not sure I even know who I am."

My mother spoke these words one afternoon as we were sorting through family pictures. Her words startled me. I resisted the impulse to quickly reply, "I know who you are. You're my mother. If there's anyone I'm certain about, it's you."

"I wanted to be a teacher," my mother continued, "but when your father and I got married, it made sense for me to quit school while he got his education, and then I got pregnant   "

She didn't finish her sentence, but I knew the rest of the story. She'd had me. And from then on, in many ways, her life was not her own. My two brothers came along, and my mom's life filled with children, church, and the predictable challenges of marriage and family.

We both were quiet for a few moments, each lost in our own thoughts. Snapshots of my mom, as real as the photos on the table in front of us, flashed through my mind:

- When I was in the sixth grade, Mom helped me write an award-winning speech, and she never tired of listening to me practice it. She knew the speech as well as, if not better than, I did.

- My mom went bowling every week with my brother as incentive for him to do his schoolwork. School was always a struggle for him, but she never stopped trying to find ways to motivate him.
- Mom let us invite all the neighborhood kids to our house on Saturday afternoons in the summer for water wars. She even filled the water balloons for us.
- Mom was always looking for ways to improve her marriage. I'll never forget overhearing my mom and her friends talk about a book called *The Total Woman*. They giggled as they contemplated greeting their husbands at the front door wrapped in nothing but cellophane!
- After my grandmother's stroke, my mom visited her in the nursing home every day on her way home from work.

I wondered if I could possibly compute the hours of cleaning, mending, and baking Mom had spent on our behalf.

"Oh, that doesn't take much talent," I imagined her saying, "not compared to what you've done. You've gone to college and graduate school. You're a professional. You've done something with your life."

This book began as my response to my mother's wonderings about who she was. You may have your own wonderings, be they fleeting or chronic. You might have lived a very different life from my mom's or from mine. Yet you've probably asked yourself, *Is this it? Am I living the life I'm meant to live? Does what I do and who I love matter?*

I have learned that when women express doubts about "who they are," they are often strangers to their own hearts and uncertain about why they were created. When women define themselves by what they do for a living, how old they are, or how they measure up to our culture's standards as reflected on glossy magazine covers, they tend to overlook what is most true about themselves—those unique qualities given to them by God. After all, when we don't know who God designed us to be, we shrink to fill the small and superficial pictures prescribed by our culture, advertising images, and media executives.

You see, I believe my mother is a hero—what I call a *braveheart*. I knew that if she articulated what she ached for, dreamed about, was willing to look like a fool for, and persistently prayed about, she would see a courageous heart for relationships. A braveheart like my mom combines courage and her God-fashioned heart for relationships to live a life of *extravagant love*.

EXTRAVAGANT LOVE

Extravagance and courage. Those are big words. Misunderstood words. And words that are intimidating in this day when women are astronauts, CEOs, and presidential candidates. We tend to think that courage is relegated to those who live big lives, overcome unbelievable difficulties, and slay dragons in their spare time. And we think that extravagance is a luxury afforded to those with grand financial resources. But extravagant love is really more a matter of the heart. It is an accumulation of moments marked by persistence, vulnerability, and discipline. It is found in rare and daily expressions of love, the speaking of truth, and the forgiveness of wrongdoing.

Extravagant love has many faces that are uniquely feminine. Women lose much (including their sense of self) when they, like my mother, discount, dismiss, and mischaracterize the brave acts they've performed in the context of relationships. "The way our culture is defining courage is so ridiculous," writes Mary Pipher in *The Shelter of Each Other*. "Courage has become *Raiders of the Lost Ark*, or riding in spaceships, killing people, taking enormous physical risks. To me, the kind of courage that's really interesting is someone whose spouse has Alzheimer's and yet manages to wake up every morning and be cheerful with that person and respectful of that person and find things to enjoy though their day is very, very difficult. That kind of courage is really undervalued in our culture."

This book is for all women who have asked questions like:

- Is what I'm doing important?
- Why am I here?
- Who was I meant to be?
- Am I doing enough?
- Is there more to life?
- What makes life worth living?

The apostle Paul describes the life of a braveheart: "Go after a life of love as if your life depended on it—because it does" (1 Corinthians 14:1, *The Message*). It's what we were made for! This is a book about women who have looked at themselves from the inside out and discovered that they are uniquely designed by God to live and love extravagantly, and who are learning to stretch courageously into demanding places with a winsome, delightful, and strong presence. That experience is what I hope for you as you read this book, put it down, read again, set it aside, pick it up again...and ponder.

I hope the stories you read in the pages ahead will encourage you to look at your own story and see that it is one worth telling, a story with clues about who you are, and a story that can propel you further into an adventure of loving extravagantly. My mother has learned, since our afternoon of sorting pictures, that her accumulated life experience is rich and deep and tells who she is. And since then she has dared to be a little more extravagant with her heart—to risk more, love more, and identify more with God, who created her to live a life of love. She now evaluates her life in light of the words of the apostle John, who urged his readers: "Let's not just talk about love; let's practice real love. This is the only way we'll know we're truly living" (1 John 3:19, *The Message*).

Sarah is a good example of the kind of women you'll read about in this book, a woman initially unsure of her heart—of who she is and what she has to offer—who is now living and loving as a braveheart. Sarah came to see me for counseling and began her first session by asking me what I lived for. When I answered that I lived for love, she laughed at me. Her laughter was not meant to be rude or unkind, but rather it reflected the hopelessness that I later observed whenever Sarah talked about anything.

Sarah sought counseling for help in losing weight. She believed she needed to lose ten to fifteen pounds, but she looked fine to me. She may have wanted to lose those few pounds that come without invitation as we approach our forties, but I guessed she really didn't need a counselor to help her with a midlife metabolic shift. Sarah was single, thirty-eight years old, and wondering a little about weight loss and a lot about the meaning of life.

When Sarah asked me what I lived for, she forced me to remember what I often forget, because I must confess that I'm a forgetful woman. I forget it's my turn to bring cookies to Bible study; I forget my best friends' birthdays, school forms, and grocery lists. But I'm also forgetful on a deeper and more damaging level than misplacing car keys and mismanaging my schedule. *I forget what I was made for.* Sometimes I get up in the morning and determine to live to lose five pounds, or to organize my closets once and for all, or to find a planner that will save me from forgotten deadlines and missed meetings. And although diets and organization can be good goals, when they become the reason for life it doesn't take long for my days to become empty and seem pointless. I suspected this was the case for Sarah.

And so I answered her question: "I live to love and be loved." And Sarah laughed. She explained matter-of-factly, "I don't think love is meant for me. And even if someone loved me, I wouldn't know how to love them back."

Sarah's answer startled me, and I looked her straight in the eyes and challenged her: "I think you're lying."

And then with fierce compassion I continued, "I think all you've ever wanted is to be loved."

We sat in silence for two or three minutes, and I watched Sarah fight to keep the dam in her heart from breaking open, but she could not win the battle this time. As tears began to stream down her face, she choked out the question, "How did you know?"

How did I know? How did I know the deepest longing of Sarah's heart was not to lose weight, but to find purpose, rest, comfort, belonging, joy, and hope in relationships? Because I'm no different from Sarah. And, I suspect, neither are you.

A Shoeless Girl

One of the abiding questions of my life is, *What should I do with my heart full of longing for relationships?* Even as a seven-year-old I knew that I wanted relationships, but that wanting required something from me and might result in rejection.

Our family moved seven times before I graduated from high school. I learned about leaving, loss, and loneliness. I also learned about being the new girl in a new school and making new friends. One of my earliest recollections is from second grade. The girls in this new school played a game during recess in which they would join hands and chant: *Tick, tock. The game is locked and nobody else can play with us. But if you do, we'll take your shoe and keep it for a week or two.*

I remember watching them play and looking down at my black-and-white Buster Brown shoes as I listened over and over to every word. I looked longingly at the girls in the game. I memorized the scene until it was their faces (instead of Dick, Jane, Sally, and Spot) that stared back at me from my second-grade reader. I hummed their tune to myself while everyone else said the Pledge of Allegiance. I waited for the glorious invitation to clasp hands and sing out the rhyming words that would signify: "I have friends. I belong. I'm part of The Girls."

I don't remember how many days I waited—it seemed like decades to a seven-year-old—until I could not possibly wait one more day. During a cold and snowy recess, I walked across the playground to greet the ringleader of The Girls. I presented her my slightly scuffed Buster Brown shoe and delivered the eloquent speech I'd practiced all the way to school: *"I want to play."*

She looked at me in amazement. To this day, I don't know if it was the fact that someone actually listened to their chant and took them at their words or if it was my undarned sock with big toe peeking through on the snowy blacktop that caused her astonished glare!

Can you recall your early experiences in relationships? Perhaps they happened in your family, on a school playground, or at a slumber party. Whatever the context, they have left indelible marks on you and contributed to what you believe about relationships. For me, after my failure to find acceptance from The Girls, I stayed at home in bed with a stomachache for the rest of the week. I pulled the covers over my head and wondered how I could ever face them again. Worse, I could not look in the mirror. I knew if I did, I would no longer see brown hair, crooked part, brown eyes, missing teeth, familiar face. I would see a shoeless being—laughed at, shunned, misunderstood. I knew something terrible must be wrong with me.

Desire for relationships—as a child, a teenager, and now as a woman—is a theme that is woven throughout my story. This desire, for me, has always felt like thirst. My longing, with satisfaction or disappointment, is a thirst I feel at the core of my being. In the psalmist's words, I thirst "as the deer pants for streams of water" (42:1). I have not always known what to do with the thirst.

For years, I believed the longings of my heart needed to be kept a secret, because I didn't know anyone else who longed for relationships as much as I did. I looked for other shoeless girls walking the hallways of my elementary school and didn't find any. And then in junior high school I began to read L. M. Montgomery's wonderful stories about the delightful exploits of Anne of Green Gables. In Volume I, page 57, I read Anne's vulnerable question and her subsequent confession:

> "Marilla," she demanded presently, "do you think that I shall ever have a bosom friend in Avonlea?"
>
> "A-a what kind of friend?"
>
> "A bosom friend—an intimate friend, you know—a really kindred spirit to whom I can confide my inmost soul. I've dreamed of meeting her all my life. I never really supposed I would, but so many of my loveliest dreams have come true all at once that perhaps this one will, too. Do you think it's possible?"

My heart burst with hope, because in Anne's amazing confession I discovered that I was not alone. Someone else spoke my language.

A HEART FULL OF LONGING

Since then I have discovered that deep within every woman is a heart full of longing for relationships. It is woven into the very fabric of the One in whose image we were made. It is a longing that whispers, "Ask me, notice me, hear me, know me, understand me, believe me, enjoy me, stay with me, care for me…and receive all of these from me as well." We long to meet others' needs and get our own needs met as well. This possibility of loving and being loved extravagantly ignites a spark in every woman's heart. We long to be loved extravagantly. We want more than ordinary relationships. We long for the extraordinary.

I imagine you picked up this book because, like me, you never give up hoping that your relationships can be richer, deeper, and more fulfilling. I meet many women when I speak at marriage and parenting seminars who have good relationships with their husbands, children, and friends, and yet long to know more about loving, to find ways to keep from settling for the mediocre, to discover fresh approaches to expressing their hearts to the people they love.

I remember one woman from Iowa who told me about a recent "Perfect Day." She'd served her husband breakfast in bed complete with his favorite motorcycle magazines to read while he ate. They took a drive in the mountains, sipped coffee in her favorite coffee shop, and she surprised him with a book about sexual intimacy that she suggested they read together to rejuvenate their love life. Her husband responded to her creative planning by listening to her attentively and sharing some of his own thoughts and feelings in a manner that was not customary for him. At the end of their day, he offered to plan a day for them together sometime in the next six months. They went to bed that night connected in a way they had not been for some time.

I laughed when this woman described to me the one difference between her and her husband's response to their Perfect Day. He fell into bed content and relieved by the intimacy they'd achieved. She lay in bed anticipating the day he would plan for them—and wondering how they could make their relationship even better! *She wanted more.*

The creativity, courage, and relentless hope of women who long for love challenges us all to understand the longing that motivates women in good, bad, and agonizing relationships to continue to want more. Just last night I was reminded of the inherent longing in a woman's heart, central to the core of her being from the day she is born.

My thirteen-year-old daughter walked into the house, ran into her room, and slammed her door. I waited a few minutes before I knocked and entered her room to find her lying on her bed, sobbing her heart out. Between sobs, she choked out her sorrows: "Life is so stressful.... I don't feel like anyone cares about things as much as I do.... All of the others girls have had boyfriends, and some have even been kissed, and I haven't even held a boy's hand. I'm afraid a boy will never like me.... And, Mom, I care about my friends so much. I want us to always be friends, and I'm afraid we'll forget each other when we change schools. Oh, Mom, what is wrong with me?"

As she wept, my longings for her almost engulfed the truth I believe passionately—the truth you will find in this book—that a woman's longing for relationships is uniquely designed by God to be her strength and glory. For a moment, I wanted to hold her close to me and protect her forever from the pain of relationships and soothe her by saying, "Don't want so much. Then you won't be disappointed." But I reminded her—and myself: "All that you are feeling right now is a sign of your strength."

She looked at me with confused disbelief as I continued, "Oh, I know it's painful, but your longings are not a sign that something is wrong with you—but that something is more profoundly right that you can possibly imagine!"

Years ago I could not have encouraged my daughter with that truth. I believed I was better off trying to suppress, silence, or eradicate my longing for relationship because reality seemed to often answer my desires with disappointment. It's easy to believe that something is wrong with us when our longings either go unmet or are challenged by husbands who fall asleep in front of the television, children who rebel, and friends who forget to return our telephone calls. Or we can just as easily convince ourselves that everyone else is to blame for the difficulties of relationships, and so we are justified in masking our longings with jealousy, anger, or withdrawal.

In her book *A Woman's Book of Life: The Biology, Psychology, and Spirituality of the Feminine Life Cycle,* Joan Borysenko, Ph.D., cites the research of those studying feminine development. The researchers suggest that the silencing of our longings begins around the age of thirteen when we realize that others can't handle our longings, that our longings get us into trouble, or that more often than not our longings go unfulfilled.

Jill came to see me for counseling when she turned sixteen. She was tired of acting out and getting into trouble. She explained to me that she started partying and behaving recklessly when her parents got divorced. She decided it was easier to leave home than to wait for her father to come back, or to wait for her family to eat dinner together, or to wait for a fairy-tale ending that would never come. She knew well what had happened to her longings when she said, "Everything good in me died when I was fifteen."

A broken family, cruel words on the playground, dateless Friday nights in high school, an unfaithful husband, a gossiping friend, a runaway daughter—all conspire to convince us that our longings must be watered down or forgotten. Or perhaps it is just the busyness of daily life or the sameness of relationships that lulls us into believing that our longings are not very practical and must be pushed aside, at least until the dishes are done!

But then something tugs at our hearts…a movie, a book, a friend, a scripture, a child, a song…and reminds us that deep within us is a desire for fulfilling relationships so intense that even the daily or disappointing realities of life cannot extinguish it. What else could motivate women to buy more than fifty million romance novels each year, to turn "chick flicks" into blockbuster movies, and to talk for hours on end to each other about relationships—not just romantic relationships but relationships with children, girlfriends, small groups, neighbors, and coworkers? An undeniable longing beckons us, urges us, haunts us, and reminds us that we were designed to experience rich, deep, passionate, and mutual relationships.

We may not disclose to anyone the full intensity of our desire, because it seems too extravagant. It's hard to admit how much we long for. It sounds too lavish, too grandiose…too much. One woman approached me at the beginning of a seminar about "Extravagant Hearts" and said, "I thought you were going to be talking about shopping at Nordstrom's." Of course, she was teasing. But her association of extravagance with high-end shopping instead of with her heart for relationships illustrates what strangers we can become to our own hearts.

How Well Do You Know Your Heart?

What do *you* want more than anything else? I ask women this question all the time. Perhaps you will find your primary longing listed among the answers that I have compiled, or maybe you, like me, find your greatest longing to be in perpetual motion and found in all of the following answers:

- A husband
- A husband who is a spiritual leader
- Children
- Children who love and serve God

- Friends
- Friends who know me and are there for me
- A family that shares my beliefs and values
- To be a size 6
- Meaningful work
- Financial security
- To never experience PMS again
- A husband who talks to me
- Children who don't talk back
- Friends who invite me for dinner
- Job security
- To skip menopause
- A dust-free house
- A maid
- A husband who doesn't snore
- Romance
- Clean cupboards

One thing is certain: Whether we long to lose weight or to find the love of our life, once a longing is fulfilled, we want something else.

A couple who recently came to see me for marriage counseling vividly illustrated the never-ending progression of a woman's longings. The first words out of the husband's mouth were "My wife has tricked me over and over again, and I can't take it anymore." When I asked more about his wife's trickery, he elaborated: "First she wanted me to go to church with her, and so I agreed and even grew to enjoy attending. Then she wanted a house with a garage, and so we saved and bought a home we both love. Then she wanted a dog, and we bought a miniature collie that I'm still not real fond of. Then she wanted a baby, and last spring we had a baby boy who is the joy of our lives. Then she wanted me to find a way to stop snoring, and so I had surgery to correct some sinus problems. Now she wants another baby—preferably a girl. I give up! Will she ever be satisfied?"

This husband expressed the exasperation of many men who have tried to make the women in their lives happy, only to conclude that a woman's longings turn her heart into an abyss that may swallow them completely. We can't really blame men for misunderstanding our hearts. Often we don't understand them either. We really believe that if we could just have what we want, then we'd be satisfied. After all, we want good things.

And so we read books on winning friends and influencing people, finding our one true love, and parenting happy and healthy children. We determine to raise our kids right, love our husbands faithfully, serve and care for our friends diligently. Why? Two reasons. First, because God created us as the life-givers, the nurturers of relationships; engaging in relationships comes naturally to us. But second, we often take on the work involved in relationships to try to satisfy our longings. Our longings become the goal of our heart's work, rather than a means to an end. And when the end is disappointing or painful, we tend to fall into one of two categories—the resigned, who live in quiet desperation, or the restless, who exist in frantic agitation.

The resigned may surrender to affairs of the heart, to anger, or to cynicism—anything to make the longings go away. The restless may be trapped in perfectionism, envy, or isolation—anything to bring the longings under control. The writer of Proverbs predicts the inevitable state of our hearts when we live only for the satisfaction of our longings: "Unrelenting disappointment leaves you heartsick" (Proverbs 13:12, *The Message*).

But now I want to lay out a far better way for you. If I speak with human eloquence and angelic ecstasy but don't love, I'm nothing but the creaking of a rusty gate.

If I speak God's Word with power, revealing all his mysteries and making everything plain as day, and if I have faith that says to a mountain, "Jump," and it jumps, but I don't love, I'm nothing.

If I give everything I own to the poor and even go to the stake to be burned as a martyr, but I don't love, I've gotten nowhere....

Love never dies. (1 Corinthians 13:1-3,8, *The Message*)

The apostle Paul explains the mysterious mix of love and longing: The fulfillment of our longings is not satisfying, but allowing our longings to lead us to a life of love never fails to satisfy. Our longings for relationships are relentless reminders of what we were made for and what is worth living for.

LIVING IN LOVE

For Personal Reflection or Discussion

1. What do you ache for, dream about, take risks for, pray to God about?

2. What dreams did you or do you have for your life?

3. Make a list of all the things you thought would make you happy, but failed to satisfy. Are you still stuck in the "I'll be happy when…" syndrome?

4. Think about your first experiences in relationships. What did they teach you about yourself and about relationships?

5. When you survey the state of your relationships today, what category best describes you?

resigned   restless   hopeful   committed

Into Action

1. Use your answers to the questions above to write a one-sentence mission statement for your life. One mission statement I wrote is: "To know God's love and embrace it heart and soul, as I go after a life of love as if my life depended on it."

2. Start looking for heroes, or *bravehearts*. Take note of ordinary acts performed faithfully or extraordinary behavior that inspires and motivates you. In my office I keep a shelf of photographs of women who model for me the life of love. You may also want to keep a scrapbook or autograph book.

CHAPTER 2

A Holy Desire

Last night while my husband and I ate a quick dinner together, something reminded us of our first year of marriage. We exchanged a series of "Remember when's…" and finished our meal smiling about our first days together so long ago.

When I got up this morning and began my quiet hour with the Lord, my mind kept wandering back to our dinner conversation. My heart felt full of love for my husband; sadness that our current busy lifestyle seems to leave little time for meandering, meaningful conversations; fear about how disconnected we can easily become. I wondered if we could structure a weekly time that would facilitate intimate conversations. I even thought about making a list of subjects to discuss.

I smiled, thinking about Dave's response if I suggested the addition of one more thing to our schedule. But I knew I would ask him anyway. (I might not show him my list of conversation topics just yet!) My resolution to ask is bolstered by a belief that the expression of my heart is not just romantic, practical, emotional, or "typically female"—it is holy.

A GIFT IN THE GARDEN

The foundational story revealing the holiness of our longing for relationships is the Genesis account of our heart's design. Often we recall the story about the creation of Eve and her disobedience in the garden as one of sin, shame, and eternal consequences; but it is also a story about design, glory, and eternal purposes. Genesis records that God created Adam first (Genesis 1:27 and 2:7), then he looked at his creation and said, "It is not good for the man to be alone. I will make a helper suitable for him" (Genesis 2:18). You remember the story: God caused a deep sleep to fall upon Adam, and while he slept God created woman out of a rib from Adam's side. When Adam awakened he exclaimed, "Bone of my bones and flesh of my flesh; she shall be called 'woman,' for she was taken out of man" (Genesis 2:23).

Have you ever pondered the chronology of these events and its implication for our design? Adam was created alone, but the woman was never alone. She was born into a relationship with Adam, designed by the Creator with relatedness as the very essence of her being. From the beginning, her awareness of her need for Adam was more conscious, more urgent, and more compelling than his awareness of his need for her. Her longing for relationship was written in her heart just as surely as her shape was formed from Adam's side.

In his translation of 1 Corinthians 11:11-13, Eugene Peterson explains the unique design and the interdependent relationship of man and woman: "Neither man nor woman can go it alone or claim priority. Man was created first, as a beautiful shining reflection of God—that is true. But the head on a woman's body clearly outshines in beauty the head of [the man]. The first woman came from man, true—but ever since then, every man comes from a woman!" *(The Message).*

The holy longing that God breathed into the woman at Creation was not only for intimacy with a man, but for all types of relationships. In his book *Men & Women*, Bible teacher and counselor Dr. Larry Crabb concludes: "Femininity, at its core, might therefore be thought of as the secure awareness of the substance [longing] God has placed within a woman's being that enables her to confidently and warmly invite others into relationship with God and with herself, knowing that there is something in each relationship to be wonderfully enjoyed."

God designed every woman with a heart full of longing, beginning with Eve who was called "the mother of all living." Theologians suggest that Eve's first name, "woman" (Genesis 2:23), describes her origin ("out of man"), while her second name, "Eve" (Genesis 3:20), points to her destiny to bring life to relationships.[1]

In fact, God uses the rest of Scripture to skillfully flesh out his design for women. If you reread the stories God tells about women, looking for this holy longing for significant relationship, you might be surprised by how deeply these stories resonate with you—so deeply that they could be your own. Well, they are. The stories of women in the Bible are all our stories: infertile Hannah, confined Esther, unwed and pregnant Tamar, widowed Ruth, jealous and vindictive Jezebel, outcast Rahab, chosen Mary, thirsty Samaritan, sick and grasping ragwoman, frantic and grieving sister, condemned adulteress, weeping and clinging prostitute. God tells their stories, in part, to reveal his unique design for women. Our longings to have babies, keep our families from danger, find a soul mate, satiate our thirst, live with purpose, heal our wounds, make a difference, survive loss, and know forgiveness are not common among women by chance. They are gifts of our feminine design.

Although men experience many of the same longings, relationships do not seem to be the vital context in which men find fulfillment of their longings. In her landmark work on feminine development, *In a Different Voice*,

Carol Gilligan notes this difference between men and women. Gilligan discovered that men express fulfillment when they achieve independence and feel strong within themselves. Women, in contrast, find fulfillment in interdependence and the development of close relationships.

IN HIS IMAGE

Not only is our longing for relationships an integral part of us, but it is also a reflection of the heart of God. God underscores Eve's uniqueness when he announces that she is being created to be a companion and helper for Adam. Our culture's understanding of the word "helper" as an inferior role couldn't be further from the truth. Scripture uses the word only two other times in the Old Testament, and both references are to God himself as our "helper" in our time of need (Psalm 10:14; Hebrews 13:6). Our design for relationships uniquely reflects God and his wondrous longing to come alongside us, hear our heart's cry, and support us in the storms of life.

Is this how you view God? In his book *Certain As the Dawn*, author and theologian Peter G. Van Breemen writes, "The fact that our view of God shapes our lives to a great extent may be one of the reasons Scripture ascribes such importance to seeking to know him."[2] Many of us view God as austere, distant, unflappable, and unmoved, but those images are not only inconsistent with his own stories, they can propel us into the mire of shame regarding our own hearts. One of the recurring conclusions women come to about their longing for relationships is that no one—husband, friend, child, coworker—cares about relationships as much as they do.

We couldn't be more wrong.

Our holy longing is a reflection of One who is simply in love with us, who longs for us more than we are capable of fully comprehending. Scripture tells us that "we love because he first loved us" (1 John 4:19). Relentless reminders of his love will eventually capture our hearts and empower us to love.

The college that I attended hosted a Valentine's banquet every February. It was the Big Event. During my freshman year I eagerly awaited an invitation to this romantic evening. I waited and waited...and waited. One week before the banquet, I still did not have a date.

Every student at this university was assigned a seat for the evening meal, and we ate our meals family-style, eight students to a table (usually four men, four women). Two days before the banquet, I exited the dining hall after the evening meal and sensed someone following me, right on my heels. Another freshman at our table, Jim, caught up to me and pulled me aside.

"W-w-would you go w-w-with me to the Valentine's banquet?" Jim asked me hesitantly.

Jim was not one of the most sought-after men on campus. My children might refer to him as "a dork." I didn't know whether to feel relief or reluctance, but I knew I would go with him. I'd been asked to the banquet!

"Yes!" I tried not to appear too eager.

"Whew," Jim sighed. "I already asked every other girl at our table."

Humiliation still floods me when I recall this story. And then I think about God's humility in light of our behavior. We try every other source of life for our relationships. We read books and attend seminars. We belittle ourselves and despise others. We cling to our independence or attach ourselves to others as if our lives depended on them. Like Jim, we ask everyone else at the table, while God waits to be our Source of life and love.

God waits patiently and humbly for thirsty women like you and me to ask him for water. He understands thirst. He so longs for a relationship with us that he asks us over and over again to be his guest at the banquet. And although he will never demand that we come, he never quits asking.

He waits eagerly for us to fall in love with him, never ashamed that he loved us first.

I caught a glimpse of God's holy longing for relationship reflected in the longing of my own mother during one of her most desperate hours. She discovered that my brother, addicted to cocaine, had stolen thousands of dollars from her bank account. The only way she could stop payment on the forged checks and hinder his purchase of more drugs was to press charges against her own son.

Tears coursed down our faces as she stood at the district attorney's desk, pen in hand, to sign the papers that would lead to an arrest warrant for her youngest son. We didn't know where he was. As she shakily signed her name, she whispered, "Where are you?" Then she did the strangest thing. She wrote on her hand.

"Mom," I asked, "what are you writing?"

She choked back her tears: "I'm writing the number of his warrant. It's all I know about him right now."

I did not know it then, but that moment in the musty, gray Jefferson County District Attorney's office was holy. Years later when I read from the prophet Isaiah, I saw that my mother's anguished actions reflected the One who said: "Can a mother forget the baby at her breast and have no compassion on the child she has borne? Though she may forget, I will not forget you! See, I have engraved you on the palms of my hands" (49:15-16).

It is impossible to overstate God's longing for us. Consider the picture of the father in Luke 15 and his daily wanting, waiting, and watching for his wayward son. The text describes their reunion: "But while he was still a long way off, his father saw him and was filled with compassion for him; he ran to his son, threw his arms around him and kissed him" (verse 20). We need only envision the sleepless father, scandalously gathering up his robes and running wildly to his son, to see the sacredness of our own longing and how it is designed to propel us into loving extravagantly.

OUR HEART'S MISSION

It has taken time and hard work for me to learn that my longings for relationships are not an end in themselves, but a means to an end—a force to lead me into an intimate relationship with God and to transform me into an extravagant lover. My holy longing compels me to seek connection, companionship, and camaraderie and also to enter the lives of others with passion.

What moves you to take cookies to the new family in your neighborhood, to send a note of encouragement to someone on the prayer list at church, to give out Popsicles to all the kids on your block, or to call a friend after a bad day at work and tell her every detail because you know she cares? Holy longing moves us to pray, bake, give, and love with abandon.

Recently, Sue came to see me for counseling, seeking help in confronting her alcoholic husband. She explained with deep regret that his heavy drinking had been a part of their marriage for more than ten years. She knew that wise intervention should have been enacted much earlier, but now it was her only hope.

I assured Sue that she was not alone. In her book *Silencing the Self,* Dana Crowley Jack cites data revealing that many women stay in an abusive relationship for an average of seven years before they even begin to talk about the realities at home. Often we read such statistics and believe they speak most articulately about the weakness of women, but I believe they actually highlight women's strength and our capacity to love in the midst of agonizing chaos.

Sue confessed to me what she believed to be her shameful weakness: "Why have I stayed with my husband? I can't eat. I can't sleep. But I cannot stop loving him." Do you hear the holy longing? When Sue began to view her longings for her husband as holy, she started making choices that revealed the awesome strength produced by her longings. She began to speak loving, powerful words to him and invite him to change. She drew comfort from the story in Hosea of God's abiding love for a wayward, stiff-necked people who would not change and turn toward him. God concedes: "My heart is changed within me; all my compassion is aroused.... Therefore I am now going to allure her; I will lead her into the desert and speak tenderly to her" (11:8; 2:14).

Sue united her family in an intervention with her husband, and they carefully and honestly allowed him to hear the terrible impact his alcoholism had on them. She requested that either he enter treatment or separate from them. Sue was sustained through tumultuous, difficult days by believing that her heart full of longing was like God's and could strengthen her courageous resolve rather than weaken it. She joined with the lover of Israel in pleading: "Return...[to me]. Your sins have been your downfall! Take words with you and return.... I will heal [your] waywardness and love [you] freely" (Hosea 14:1-2,4).

Because Sue was no longer ashamed of her love and her longing for her husband, she joined Al-Anon, a support group for people with alcoholic loved ones, while she waited for her husband to enter and persevere in the difficult days of early sobriety. She found shelter in the lives of others with stories similar to hers. While Sue's husband completed treatment at an inpatient facility, Sue did her own hard work in individual and group counseling to ensure that her heart was strengthened in its resolve to love her husband fully but to never go back to the destructive life they had slid into.

On Palm Sunday morning, one year into their recovery process, Sue shared a homily with her church family. Courageously and with her husband's permission, Sue decided that she could disclose the secret struggles of her family in the context of her new understanding of her own holy longing and of God's even greater longing for her and her husband.

The overwhelmingly positive response of the congregation brought new life to Sue's relationships in the church and a deeper faith in the reality of the Resurrection and the One who makes all things new (Revelation 21:5). Several families determined to become actively involved in supporting Sue and her husband. Four couples now meet once a week to pray together and offer support. And as a result of Sue and her husband's vulnerability, one other couple in the church with a marriage in peril has come forward to ask for help.

Not every story has a happy ending. But I believe Sue would tell you that the miracle of change has not only been for her husband, but for herself as well. She has become stronger in her convictions, bolder in her invitations to others, more authentic in her relationships, and more alive in her daily walk with God.

You see, the holy longing invites change, promotes growth, and calls us to relationships that are life-giving. God uniquely designed women to carry the water of life that enables relationships to flourish, while at the same time giving everyone who comes into relationship with them a thirst for Jesus, the Living Water. Is it any wonder that the Enemy seeks to silence this holy longing?

Which brings us back to Sarah, the woman who laughed at the idea of living for love. Surrender to the holiness of her longing for relationships compelled her to drop her defenses and enter into new ways of relating by making courageous choices and significant changes. When Sarah acknowledged the deepest longings of her heart, she could no longer remain paralyzed by a frozen heart. But the thawing of her heart did mean she felt more pain and sorrow as she became aware of her present loneliness and longing for relationships.

Such sorrow need not be a catalyst for despair; it can be a doorway to hope. Sarah joined a singles group in her church, no longer ashamed of her single status or angry that she must play an active part in relationships for them to flourish, but instead feeling a kinship with other single men and women and with God.

Sarah has found intimacy with God as she has come to see him as One who longs and waits for relationships with an even greater intensity than she does. She knows that she must seek out the solace of his company with an intensity equal to her longing for human relationships so that he can sustain her when involving herself with others does not work out well. She has also signed up for a creative writing class at a community college, believe her longing will only increase her creative juices. I, for one, cannot wait to read what she writes!

Sarah now ends almost every counseling session by teasing me and reminding me, and herself: "All I've ever wanted is to be loved." And she laughs—a wonderful, heartfelt laugh.

She reminds me of another Sarah, the Sarah of the Old Testament who longed for a child. When God promised her one at a ridiculously old age, she, too, laughed. Her laughter was not out of hope or joy...at first. But later, after watching the strange ways of God unfold and eventually surrendering to his promise, she praised God and named her son Isaac, which means "laughter."

The woman who accepts her holy longing for relationships from the hands of a loving, longing Creator can laugh with delight at his promises. While she is unsure of how or when they may be fulfilled, she is certain that not only does God know "the secrets of [her] heart" (Psalm 44:21), but a passionate longing for relationships is the secret of his heart as well.

L I V I N G I N L O V E

For Personal Reflection or Discussion

1. What kinds of things does your longing for relationship compel you to want/do?

2. What makes your heart sing?

3. Up to this point, how have you characterized your desire for relationships?

desperate	pitiful	embarrassing
holy	sacred	emotional
unimportant	primary	burdensome
unique	Christlike	wonderful
shameful	exhilarating	other _____

4. How could viewing your longing for relationships as holy, change how you interact in your current relationships? Consider some specific situations and the different responses that could unfold if your perspective were different.

Into Action

1. Look for stories in the Bible that tell about God's longing for relationships and spend time meditating on them. Here are some passages to get you started:

Genesis 3	Isaiah 49	Hosea
Luke 15	1 Timothy 2	Revelation 3

2. Next time you get angry with yourself for wanting relationships or doubt your value in relationships, imagine Christ visiting with you. What view would he have of you? What might he say to you?

CHAPTER 3

Loving from a Whole Heart

Our longings are designed to be a source of strength, a compass in the storms of difficult relationships, and a wondrous reflection of the heart of God. But many women don't know their God-given longings are their strength so they bury or ignore this compass and lose their way.

I wish I could tell you that I've always pursued honorable ways of handling my longings. But along the way I've become tired, discouraged, and afraid. People weren't always nice and friendly. For that matter, neither was I. And I was getting impatient for my longings to be fulfilled in ways I thought I wanted.

As a young adult, I discovered something that numbed my longings and offered an escape from figuring out what to do with my full heart. I decided that my longing for relationships was not something holy, but something horrible. I became more and more certain that it would only lead me into disappointment and loneliness, so I chose to habitually anesthetize my longings with alcohol. Of course, then I had another problem.

Many years later, when I first began to look at my life honestly and acknowledge that my addiction to alcohol was an escape from the difficulties of relationships, I felt a sense of emptiness inside. But over time I discovered that, as God's child, I had inherited both his design and his

What a relief! God designed me for the relationships I desired, so there was no shame in wanting those desires to be fulfilled. And he'd given me the resources to love and be loved truly, madly, and deeply.

I hope the rest of this book will help you discover your heart full of holy desire as the key to a life filled with extravagant love. You can be an extravagant lover—a woman of courage, creativity, generosity, compassion, desire, and relentless hope—no matter the state of your relationships. Extravagant loving begins with identifying the ways in which you spend your heart's energy.

THE TENSION OF RELATIONSHIPS

The tension of relationships is a strand in the fabric of every woman's story. Tension is the constant balancing of opposing forces that lies at the heart of every relationship. Wanting and waiting. Longing and fulfillment. Happiness and hurt. Emptiness and gratification. Water and thirst. Acceptance and rejection. Hope and disappointment. Love and loss. Where does this tension come from?

The entrance of sin into the human condition introduced the tension into relationships. Dr. Dan Allender, in his book *Intimate Allies*, writes about the importance of the Creation story in the Bible:

> The first three chapters of the Bible tell a dramatic story. It is the story of a perfect creation, the offer of inconceivable joy, the wild meeting of two people—who were once one, who became two, and who then longed to join again in union—a devastating fall into evil, a divine rescue, and provision for restoration. This story tells me all I ultimately need to know to grasp the simplicity and complexity of life. It sets the tone and direction of the entire Bible.

God explained the future course of relationships, apart from future redemption, when he gently, but firmly, announced to Adam and Eve the awful consequences of their disobedience. God's judgment on his children reached the core of their design. God explained that Eve would know pain in childbearing (Genesis 3:16). The glory of her design would also bring her much hurt. I imagine that God spoke these words with the infinite sorrow of One who knew the anguish of which he was speaking.

This prophecy of the tension between joy and pain extends to us today not only in the literal birthing of children, but also in the joy and pain of bearing relationships. We all know the reality of hoping for a relationship to begin, watching it take shape, nourishing it expectantly, and groaning and cheering during the inevitable ups and downs of its life.

When sin entered the Garden of Eden, God himself experienced desire and disappointment, fellowship and loneliness as a result of Adam and Eve's rebellion. In the New Testament, Christ expresses his desire and disappointment in relationships with uniquely feminine imagery: "Jerusalem! Jerusalem!… How often I've ached to embrace your children, the way a hen gathers her chicks under her wings, and you wouldn't let me" (Matthew 23:37, *The Message*).

Simply put, relationships are wonderful and painful; they are what we were made for, but they are sometimes out of our reach. They quench our thirst for a moment, but leave us thirsty for more.

Wondrously, even in the midst of the tragic choices in the garden, God already had a plan for redemption. *The Expositor's Bible Commentary* states: "In the pain of the birth of every child, there was to be a reminder of the hope that lay in God's promise. Birthpangs are not merely a reminder of the futility of the Fall, they are as well a sign of impending joy." In the New Testament, Paul describes this pain and promise: "We know that the whole creation has been groaning as in the pains of childbirth right up to the present time. Not only so, but we ourselves...groan inwardly as we wait eagerly for our adoption as sons, the redemption of our bodies. For in this hope we were saved" (Romans 8:22-24).

Right now we live "in the meantime," between the reality of Eden and the hope of heaven. I believe that learning to love with a whole heart in the meantime is our life's work.

How Do You Handle the Tension?

How have you coped with the inevitable tension that is in relationships? Your answer reveals how you spend the energy of your heart. The energy of the heart consists of your passions, desires, and motivations. We are describing the energy of the heart when we say, "She did a halfhearted job" or "She put all of her heart into it." The energy of your heart is defined by what you believe about yourself, others, and God. And what you believe is revealed by what you do with the tension of relationships.

The following statements may be clues to where you direct the energy of your heart. Have you ever said or thought any of the following statements?

- I don't need friends.
- People can't be trusted.
- If he/she doesn't love me, I can't go on.
- I won't give up.
- I'm too busy for friends.
- What I'm feeling is not a big deal.
- I'm not as gifted as others are.
- I'd better take care of myself—no one else will.
- It's better to be safe than sorry.
- My problems are nothing compared to other people's problems.

- I don't know how to express myself.
- If anyone really knew me, they wouldn't like me.
- I shouldn't expect so much.
- God is all I need.

Each of the above statements requires heart energy—thought, determination, effort—to live out. For example, the idea that I don't need friends requires the belief that I am sufficient, the determination to not want anything from anyone, and the effort to live independently of others. When the energy of my heart is devoted to living apart from others, I have little energy left to engage in relationships. Of course, we can just as easily spend our heart's energy on becoming too dependent on others, belittling ourselves, or becoming completely self-absorbed. The energy of the heart is not an unlimited resource, so it is wise to evaluate where we spend it.

While writing this book, I am privileged to look at the tension of relationships through the eyes of my adolescent daughter. Sometimes it is particularly painful to revisit this world of best friends, braces, and boys with changing voices.

Kristin got in the car one day after school last week, and I could tell it had been a bad day. The PE teacher had chosen two captains to pick teams for flag football. Kristin stood with increasing humiliation as almost everyone in the class was picked for a team before she was. In fact, when only Kristin and another girl were left to be picked, the teacher suggested they just choose whichever team they wanted, in an attempt to end their misery.

As Kristin told me about this familiar, cruel-and-unusual rite of passage, she concluded, "The worst part was that my friends just looked at me and didn't try to get me picked for their team!" She continued, "I hate this feeling of wanting something and not being able to do anything about it. I wish I could just cut it out of my heart."

Oh, I know what she means. But what we do with that tension of longing but not getting determines where we spend our heart's energy and directly influences the quality of our relationship with ourselves, others, and God. Like Kristin, we may believe that attacking our longings is the only way to make it in this world. We may despise ourselves, withdraw from others, or blame God. We may take matters into our own hands and attempt to manipulate and scheme ourselves into the relationships we desire. Or we may simply settle apathetically for the status quo, wanting more in our relationships but not knowing how to make it happen. The energy of our heart is so easily misspent and quickly becomes unavailable for wholeheartedly engaging in a life of love.

An Undivided Heart

Before our hearts can be free to love extravagantly they must be whole hearts, not debilitated by "desires that battle within [us]" (James 4:1). My father-in-law suffered from physical heart disease for over thirty years, but did not detect it until the damage was irreparable. When heart pains sent him to the emergency room, he was shocked to learn that only 30 percent of his heart was functioning. He spent the next fifteen years regulating his diet, exercising, and undergoing several medical procedures, including two open-heart surgeries.

Sadly, like my father-in-law, we may walk around with a heart for relationships that is similarly diseased and deadened, living far below the level at which we were designed to function, without even realizing it. Physician and author Paul Pearsall has studied the physical heart and what promotes healing and growth after heart attacks. In *The Heart's Code*, he writes that understanding the energy of your heart toward yourself and others can "not only save and prolong life, but make our life and all of the life around us more hardy—and 'hearty'—for everyone and everything."[1]

The psalmist prayed: "Teach me your way, O LORD, and I will walk in your truth; give me an undivided heart" (Psalm 86:11). The best way to detect a divided heart is to hold it up to the example of a whole heart that Jesus gives in the Gospels: "An expert in the law tested [Jesus] with this question: 'Teacher, which is the greatest commandment in the Law?' Jesus replied: '"Love the Lord your God with all your heart.... Love your neighbor as yourself." All the Law and the Prophets hang on these two commandments'" (Matthew 22:35-40).

The woman with a whole heart lives with the tension of relationships when she esteems herself by agreeing with God that what he has made is "very good" (Genesis 1:31), and when she lives with a passionate desire for relationships but does not demand them. She can do this only because she is depending on God to be her Source of life.

In subsequent chapters we will be looking at many ways to strengthen our hearts to obey this greatest commandment. But before we go too much further, it might be good to meet a real-life woman who is wholly engaged in the life of love; she'll give us a picture of what we're aiming for.

ONE WOMAN'S JOURNEY

During the time that Jill, the sixteen-year-old I told you about earlier, came to see me for counseling, we decided to bring her mother into the counseling process. Jill's mother, Darlene, was angry, tired, confused, and scared to death that her daughter was headed for serious trouble. She looked at me with weary eyes and asked, "What should I do?"

When I asked Darlene what *she* thought she should do, I knew that her answer of dismay and confusion came from a life filled with work, worries, and mounting problems. I asked her to reserve one hour a day for herself—away from her children, the evening news, and all the other demands for her time and attention—in order to listen to her own heart.

Listening to your heart may sound like a mysterious, New Age, self-indulgent practice. Christian women sometimes believe that living a life of love requires that we forget ourselves, ignore our desires, and take care of everyone else first. But Scripture reminds us that "above all else" we should understand our own heart, because it is the only way to guard it and turn it into a gushing wellspring of life (Proverbs 4:23)!

After one week of setting aside an hour for herself, Darlene asked me, "So what am I supposed to do in this hour? How is this going to help me help Jill?"

Being quiet is hard. Minutes seem like hours, and our minds wander everywhere from meal planning to counting the flowers in the wallpaper pattern. But quietness allows us to be attentive to ourselves and to listen to our hearts like a caring parent, a loving spouse, or a faithful friend would. I asked Darlene to think about her needs, wants, motives, thoughts, feelings, and intuitive "hunches" with regard to herself, Jill, and their life together. I asked her to sense what was stirring within her, to identify it, name it, and to guard against disowning or silencing her inner longings.

Darlene came in a week later and said, "This may sound crazy…" (when we're not used to listening to our hearts, it can be terrifying to admit the depth of our longing) "but what I really want to do is quit my job and spend a year with Jill. We could homeschool, work on projects together, and explore some of the historical landmarks in our area."

I must admit, her idea did sound a little crazy to me too. After all, Darlene was a single mom, and her family needed her income to survive. Jill was an angry, rebellious teenager, and I was not sure the idea of spending a

year away from her friends with her mom would be very appealing. Darlene admitted that the year together might be just what they needed or it
might just be a catastrophe. I suggested to Darlene that she continue listening to her heart, knowing that in quietness she would find her strength
(Isaiah 30:15).

As Darlene continued to reserve quiet time for herself, she reflected on
her own childhood. (Listening to your heart can include reliving fearful
and painful experiences and examining your strategies to silence your heart
so you never have to feel that anguish again.) Darlene recalled her own
mother, who suffered from chronic depression and would often withdraw
from the family into her bedroom for days at a time. Darlene wondered if
her own resistance to reserving time for herself came from resenting her
mother's frequent absences.

She then remembered the many afternoons and weekends she would
spend at her grandmother's house, baking cookies, making art projects, and
working in the garden. She thought about the comfort, nurture, and security her grandmother's presence brought into her life. Her memories gave
her greater confidence that what she longed to give Jill—an extravagant
dose of her presence during this tumultuous time—might not be such a
crazy idea after all.

Darlene confided to me that she had begun to pray about taking a year
to pour herself into her daughter. I watched in delight as Darlene's quiet
time was building her faith. Remembering increases our faith, and faith
gives our longings purpose. Darlene decided it was time to give feet to her
plan.

Darlene approached her pastor with her yearlong plan for herself and
her daughter and asked if the church had any resources available to help
them financially. Darlene admitted that making this request required more
vulnerability and humility than she had ever experienced before. The

pastor expressed his respect for Darlene and promised to find financial support for her and Jill during Darlene's "sabbatical."

As I marveled at Darlene's courage and heart full of love for her daughter, I was reminded that listening to our own hearts compels us to listen to God's heart for us. Darlene's unabashed longing for her daughter took her into the heart of the One whose love doesn't falter. I didn't need to tell Darlene that she was embarking on a wild, unpredictable journey and that she would need to believe that there is One who loves her with greater extravagance than she is loving her own daughter.

Loving with a whole heart requires an openness to God's extravagant love. You will never find a lover who will adore, desire, embrace, and delight in you more than God does. As you love with a whole heart, you will hear his lovely longing with sweeter and deeper understanding as he pleads with vulnerability and humility: "Behold, I stand at the [heart's] door and knock; if any [woman] hears My voice and opens the door, I will come in [and fellowship with her] and [she] with me" (Revelation 3:20, NASB). What a relief to discover One who understands our heart full of longing! God's longing and love for us becomes a merciful model for extravagantly loving others.

When Darlene revealed her plan to Jill, she was furious. She shouted at her mother, "You are going to ruin my life!" Darlene was not discouraged by Jill's response because she had already meditated on the reality of "constraining love": "For the love of Christ constraineth us; because we thus judge, that...he died for all, that they which live should not henceforth live unto themselves" (2 Corinthians 5:14-15, KJV). Darlene knew that God's love for her constrained, or compelled, him to give up the life of his Son and that her love for Jill required her to give up her life for her daughter. Darlene believed that Jill would not be able to resist the concerted effort of two such extravagant lovers!

Darlene "lost" a year of her life and won her daughter. She also gained a year of experiences with God that she wouldn't trade for anything. She would tell you that she knows who God designed her to be, she likes herself, and she is more confident in other relationships. In fact, Darlene attracts mothers from all over the city who want to know what she did to bring about such radical change in her family. Darlene tells them that there were lots of valleys, discouraging days, and enormous challenges. She also tells them that living extravagantly out of the fullness of her heart is invigorating!

Darlene is a woman who is more alive than anyone I know. She speaks out, takes risks, and makes a practice of surprising her daughter with adventures for the two of them. In December, Darlene and Jill made and filled more than one hundred Christmas stockings for a local rescue mission.

Jill will go to college in the fall. She is no longer shut down and angry. She wants to study psychology, but she will tell you that more than anything else she wants to be like her mother—the woman who saved her life!

Darlene has returned to work, but she has not stopped spending her daily quiet hour praying and planning for how she will continue to love extravagantly. She prays that her "love may abound more and more in knowledge and depth of insight," that she "will be filled with the fruit of righteousness that comes through Jesus Christ—to the glory and praise of God" (Philippians 1:9-11).

When I think of Darlene, I am reminded of Frederick Buechner's description in *Now and Then* of James Muilenburg, his Old Testament professor in seminary.

He was a fool in the sense that he didn't or couldn't or wouldn't resolve, intellectualize, evade the tensions of his faith but lived those tensions out, torn almost in two by them at times. His faith was not a seamless garment but a ragged garment with the seams showing, a garment that he clutched about him like a man in a storm.

Muilenburg was a fool, I suppose, in the sense that he was an intimate of the dark, yet held fast to the light as if it were something you could hold fast to; in the sense that he wore his heart on his sleeve even though it was in some ways a broken heart…. A fool, in other words, for Christ.[2]

WHAT WILL YOU CHOOSE?

Darlene's story illustrates that living in love requires intentional, thoughtful, courageous choices—choices that are lived out in the practical moments of everyday life. The apostle John encourages us: "My dear children, let's not just talk about love; let's practice real love" (1 John 3:18, *The Message*).

Our hearts have only so much energy, or passion, and we make thousands of conscious and subconscious decisions about where our passion will be spent. When we say "yes" to meeting a friend for lunch, watching *ER* on Thursday night television, or helping a child with his homework, we are allocating our passion by our choices. When we say "no" to cleaning out the hall closet, spending an hour in quiet prayer and reflection, or playing Monopoly with our kids, we are reserving our passion by our decisions. Our choices to allocate and reserve passion form patterns of behavior that become ingrained in our daily lives.

Some patterns of behavior are life-giving and healthy, like daily exercise, devotions, and a cup of coffee from Starbucks (okay, I just threw that one in because it's a habit I don't want to give up!). Other patterns may start out incidentally or innocently, but become destructive because they drain our hearts of passion for righteous relationships with God, others, and ourselves.

A choice to pursue a relationship with a certain individual, to end a relationship, to engage in an activity, to drop out of something, to go on a diet, or to partake of food or drink can become a pattern of behavior that absorbs our energy, kidnaps our passion, and takes us away from what we were made for. Jesus simply reminds us: "Where your treasure is [where you spend your passion], there your heart will be" (Matthew 6:21).

During the complexity, pain, and busyness of life, our deepest longing—our holy longing for relationship with God and others—is often dismissed, supplanted, or kidnapped by unhealthy relationships, activities, or ideas that keep us from being free to love with a whole heart. The songwriter croons that we keep "looking for love in all the wrong places." The Scriptures warn: "Be careful, or you will be enticed to turn away and worship other gods and bow down [surrender your hearts] to them" (Deuteronomy 11:16).

Passion always goes somewhere. In the next section of this book, we will consider some of the life-directions, or gods, that entice us, steal our passion, and keep us from loving extravagantly. When life is disappointing, boring, rewarding, or lonely, and these life-directions seduce you, what will you choose? What patterns of behavior are second nature to you? What captures your heart?

It is humbling to acknowledge that our choices to be occupied with dieting, perfectionism, gossip, certain relationships, and a host of other unhealthy activities keep us from what we long for most: meaningful relationships with others and a vibrant, life-giving relationship with God. Saint Augustine once said that God is always trying to give good things to us, but our hands are too full to receive them. Not only our hands, but our hearts!

In the chapters ahead you will read stories that I hope will resonate with you deeply—stories about women who have been hurt and abused; about women who have made mistakes and foolish choices; about women who are in good marriages and who are cultivating healthy friendships; about persistent women who read books about love, hoping for still more in their relationships; about women who lead ordinary lives and in the midst of them make brave choices to love wildly, relentlessly, extravagantly.

Quite simply, these are stories about the most important work in the Kingdom—loving. "Whoever lives in love lives in God, and God in [her]" (1 John 4:16).

LIVING IN LOVE

For Personal Reflection or Discussion

1. How much time do you spend caring for yourself? What do you do to take care of yourself? If you don't set aside time for yourself, why not?

2. Is spending time alone hard for you? Why? What could you do to reserve time for yourself?

3. How has your past shaped your beliefs about yourself and your relationships? Recall specific events, interactions, and feelings. What imprints from past experiences do you see on present behavior?

Into Action

1. Ask a few friends to describe you in a single sentence and record their statements on a piece of paper. What do their descriptions suggest about the ways you handle the tension of relationships?

2. One way to listen to God's heart for you is to read John 19 (a picture of Christ's whole heart for us) every day for a month. Meditating on God's extravagant choice on our behalf informs and strengthens our choices in relationships. I began this discipline over two years ago, and it has revolutionized my love life—not only with God, but with others as well.

PART II

THE CAPTIVE HEART

CHAPTER 4

The Queen of Hearts

She was fifteen minutes late. My friend Emily and I sat in Starbucks, waiting for another friend to meet us for coffee, and she was late. If the truth be told, our friend Diane was often late.

The three of us had planned this time together a month earlier. We had all agreed that we didn't see each other enough because of our busy schedules, so we committed to meeting once a month for at least an hour to catch up on our lives and spend time nurturing our friendship. On this particular morning, we'd planned for only an hour together, and Diane had already missed a quarter of our time.

Emily checked her watch and groaned, "Diane's chronic lateness feels so disrespectful. It doesn't seem like she cares very much about us or our friendship. I think I'm going to say something to her."

I spied Diane's car pulling into the parking lot and something in me froze. We had only about forty minutes left, and I didn't want to spend it discussing a subject that might be unpleasant. I urged Emily, "Diane probably has a good excuse. She almost always does. Remember the time her son dropped his ant farm in the kitchen…"

Diane rushed into the coffee shop, and we all exchanged hugs and greetings. I anticipated Diane's apology, but none came. She excused herself to order a coffee drink, and Emily and I looked at each other. We were two friends at a standoff: Emily was frustrated by our friend's lateness and hurt by its impact on our friendship, and I wanted to ignore Diane's late arrival in order to maintain the facade of perfect peace and harmony within our relationship.

So who's the controlling woman. Emily or me? Actually we both are.

Emily likes order. She spends a lot of energy finding, developing, and sticking to standards for judging what is good and bad, right and wrong. She imposes these standards upon herself first and works diligently to always keep them. She is often hard on herself and ashamed of her own imperfections. Emily is a loyal, conscientious friend and has a keen sense of judgment. In this case, she was right to take note of Diane's chronic late-ness, and it could have been loving for us to ask Diane to show more respect for our time together. But Emily can also impose her high standards unfairly on others. When a person has weaknesses and makes mistakes, Emily becomes frustrated and disappointed, which can be reflected as self-righteousness or a negative, critical spirit. Emily often laments that she has few friends and that people seem intimidated by her.

I, on the other hand, like happiness and harmony. I spend too much energy avoiding pain and working to ensure that everyone likes me and is never uncomfortable. I want a controlled environment where there are no hurt feelings, no injustices, and no conflicts. As a result I often sacrifice my own well-being for the sake of avoiding conflict. I also tend to overlook the failures of others in order to keep the peace, instead of using failure to deepen and strengthen relationships by bringing it out into the light and allowing conviction, repentance, and change to occur. I often feel like I do "all the work" of relationships and secretly harbor anger and hurt.

Both Emily and I have a tendency to spend our heart's energy in efforts to attain the unattainable: a controlled world filled with perfect people where we are never disappointed or uncomfortable. Rather than surrender to an uncontrollable God who made us and trust him during the ups and downs of relationships, we take control by directing the energy of our hearts in ways that allow us to feel as if we're at the steering wheel of our own lives.

I call the woman determined to stay in control "the Queen of Hearts." When control becomes the life force of the heart, it gradually takes over. Its goal is to rule in every room. It eventually empties every chamber of the heart of vitality for meaningful relationships. It refuses to acknowledge weakness, it is ashamed of failure, it is energized by pretense, and it flees from sorrow.

The Scriptures poignantly describe a controlling woman: "In her heart she boasts, 'I sit as queen; I am not a widow [even though her husband is dead], and I will never mourn'" (Revelation 18:7). Control is a multi-faceted monarch that can use up every ounce of heart energy for relationships. Many women do not realize that one reason they struggle with relationships is that the Queen of Hearts has taken them captive.

In this chapter we will look at three life-directions of controlling women: independence, infatuation, and idealism. When any of these three becomes the compass that directs us through the storms, the fog, or the calm of relationships, we will end up lost and living apart from our true design.

INDEPENDENCE: I AM WOMAN, HEAR ME ROAR

When independence becomes the life force of the heart, the result is a determination never to be vulnerable, needy, or burdensome. The energy of the heart is expended to keep people at a distance and often looks for an excuse to be more focused on tasks than on relationships.

Just last night I was reminded of the ease with which I can cripple my own heart for relationships. All day long I'd looked forward to my husband's homecoming and anticipated a time of conversation and connection with him. I longed to talk about our son's struggles in math, our daughter's upcoming dance at school, a conversation I'd had with a mutual friend, a book I was reading about how to plan a life-changing vacation! But things didn't work out as I'd anticipated.

Dave arrived home later than expected, and I greeted him with guarded eagerness for our evening together (my controlling heart was already wincing at his tardiness). We ate dinner amidst the usual chaos our family of four brings to the dinner table. After dinner our children went their separate ways, and I began the hoped for conversation: "So, how was your day?"

"Stressful," Dave replied. "I need to put a new washer on the sink in the bathroom upstairs. Better get to it."

Before I could even respond, he was gone. I felt overlooked, cheated, and foolish for ever anticipating a satisfying conversation. He hadn't even asked about my day! With lightning-like speed I consoled myself and brought my heart under control: "I don't even *want* to talk to him now."

Later in the evening when Dave was ready for a conversation, I retaliated: "I need to fold the laundry. Better get to it."

Whether it's because of the inevitable paper cuts or staggeringly deep wounds of relationships, we diminish our potential for relationships when we determine that the only way to soothe ourselves is not to want relationships, to live independently of others. Believing that we don't need, don't want, or shouldn't expect much from relationships siphons vitality from our hearts and prevents us from loving with abandon as God does.

So what do we miss when we distance ourselves from relationships, other than pain and further disappointment? In my interaction with Dave, I went from being a hopeful, vibrant woman to a sarcastic, deadened woman. I used my hurt and anger at not getting what I wanted on my terms to cut myself off from a subsequent invitation that might have resulted in a meaningful conversation. Instead of being open to Dave and our relationship, I wounded him and hurt myself further. And I ended up with the laundry!

INFATUATION: I CAN'T LIVE WITHOUT YOU

Cutting off desire is not the only way we enfeeble our heart for relationships. Demanding and manipulating others to satisfy us is equally controlling and destructive. We may believe that without a particular relationship we can't survive, so we're willing to do anything or become anyone to establish and maintain that relationship. Controlling women cling unhealthily to relationships when they won't "share" friendships, when they demand that their own needs be attended to first, or when they nurse the inevitable slights of relationships into life-threatening injuries.

I worked with a woman in my counseling practice who bravely agreed to allow me to write about her. Jan and her husband joined their church soon after visiting it for the first time. Jan looked forward to meeting friends and becoming a part of the fellowship of women in the church. She especially liked the pastor's wife. But when Jan discovered that the pastor's wife had many friends, she began to feel hopeless of ever being a part of the "inner circle" of women.

During one Wednesday night prayer meeting, Jan requested prayer for unspecified health problems. Several of the women expressed concern after the church service, including the pastor's wife. With little thought about the consequences, Jan expanded her story to the point that she confided to the pastor's wife that she had cancer, even though that was not the case.

For a while, her story hooked the pastor's wife, and she called Jan frequently expressing concern and curiosity about Jan's health. But over time, it appeared to Jan that her new friend's interest subsided. Jan responded by making her story more desperate and dramatic, until it reached a point where the women in the church began to doubt Jan's honesty.

The pastor's wife kindly confronted Jan about her story and Jan panicked. Fortunately, she had enough integrity and courage to seek help in counseling. She eventually told the women of the church the truth, sought forgiveness, opened the door to genuine relationships, and waited for those friendships to develop naturally over time.

Clinging to others in infatuation as well as withdrawing from others in independence deplete the heart of the resources of trust and openness that are necessary for a life of love. Healthy relating requires that we live with desire, but without demand.

With my longing for a conversation with my husband, I might pray about an opportunity as well as pray about my disappointment when the opportunity fails to materialize. Demanding would sharpen the useless skills of nagging and pouting, while praying would channel my desire into a more intimate relationship with God that could overflow into my relationship with my husband.

I could also send an invitation to Dave or leave a note at the dinner table asking him for time to talk. Then my desire will spark creativity and shape me into an inviting woman. Demanding, on the other hand, would guarantee that I become a boring and bitter woman. Staying in touch with my desire will open my heart to trust and flexibility. Demanding would shut down my heart and inevitably leave me alone, folding the laundry.

Idealism: Somewhere over the Rainbow

Idealism is a charming tyrant that rules the heart and robs it of the energy necessary to love extravagantly. *Webster's Dictionary* defines idealism as "of or relating to perfection." Many Christian women like you and me unwittingly allow idealism to control them because it seems to bring order to their lives and looks so appealing. We think, *If I could simply make myself and the people and things around me just so, my life will be in order.*

In her book *Traveling Mercies*, writer Anne Lamott describes her struggle with idealism: "I believed if I could just do a little better, I would finally have the things I longed for—a sense of OKness and connection and meaning...that I would be loved someday. I was thirty-five when I discovered that a B-plus was a really good grade."

Lamott concludes: Idealism "will keep you insane your whole life."[1] Writer and theologian Oswald Chambers similarly warns in *My Utmost for His Highest:* "The ideal may actually lull us into ruin."[2]

We are going to examine the heart ruled by idealism from the outside in, looking at it more closely than we did independence and infatuation, because it is more subtle and slippery than the other two. It's easy to miss.

The following statements reveal a heart under the dominion of idealism. When idealism regulates the heart, it is not free to offer extravagant love.

- I seem to be the only person in my family who knows how to keep things clean.
- If I lose my temper with my children, I am a bad mom.
- There is a right way and a wrong way to do everything.
- My prayer life is never good enough.
- It is very important that everyone likes me.

- If others think I am a failure, then I am a failure.
- If I make mistakes, others will not approve of me.
- It would be terrible if I were late.
- If I don't stay thin, no one will ever be attracted to me.
- If I am discouraged or have a bad day, others will perceive me as weak.
- It is my responsibility to correct others when they make a mistake.
- If I check and double-check my work, I can make sure it is perfect.
- I can prevent my children from getting sick if I am very diligent in caring for them.
- I can control whether others like me by being careful how I say things to them.
- My friends should never be late.
- My children should always do what I tell them to do.
- I should be able to anticipate problems before they occur.
- If I send my husband to the grocery store, he will probably get the wrong things.
- I don't like others to buy me gifts because they couldn't possibly know what I want.

A woman who spends her heart's energy on idealism will be caught up in appearance, control, and legalism rather than being free to love others with abandon.

The Facade of Outward Appearance

Idealism often first asserts control with an obsession about outward appearance. The prophet Isaiah described women of his day who were obsessed with appearance:

The women of Zion are haughty, walking along with outstretched necks, flirting with their eyes, tripping along with mincing steps, with ornaments jingling on their ankles…bangles and headbands and crescent necklaces, the earrings and bracelets and veils, the headdresses and ankle chains and sashes, the perfume bottles and charms, the signet rings and nose rings, the fine robes and the capes and cloaks, the purses and mirrors, and the linen garments and tiaras and shawls. (Isaiah 3:16-23)

The prophet lists twenty-one items of apparel the women used to cover themselves. He wasn't decrying the efforts of these women to look nice or stylish, but rather their attempt to create a facade. The prophet proclaims to the women of his day that the energy they've spent on keeping up appearances has left them empty and destitute (3:26).

Such obsession with appearance has only gotten worse since the time of Isaiah. Outward attractiveness, having it all together, and looking good are all prized ideals in our culture—even our Christian culture. Over the past few years I have talked and counseled with hundreds of women of all shapes, sizes, and looks, and I've discovered:

- Very few of us are satisfied with our looks. (By "looks" I mean our physical appearance, the "look" of our family, our overall presentation to others.)
- Many of us look good on the outside but still struggle with self-esteem and a sense of self-worth.
- The majority of us feel trapped in a cycle of always trying to look good and never feeling as if we've succeeded.

Appearance obsession is a chronic, painful way of life that keeps us preoccupied instead of engaged in authentic relationships. When we are focused on external ideals, we may deny or overlook internal realities, both good and bad.

For example, as my addiction to alcohol developed, I became more intensely concerned with "keeping it all together." I was frantic to put up a good image because I didn't want anyone to guess that I might have a real problem, and I didn't want to look at the problem either. With the energy of my heart consumed by trying to look good, I didn't have any energy to look deeply into my own heart.

At the same time, my relationships with others were not genuine. The foundation of my relationships was built on my persona or image, not on the real me. I believed others would be shocked or disgusted if they knew the real me. This assumption allowed me to harbor anger and hurt at others whom I perceived as having "failed" me; the truth is, they didn't really know me.

And I was mad at God. I knew he saw the truth beneath the facade, but I believed he would love me only if I tried harder to cover the truth, to put on a good show, to not become an embarrassment to him.

And then I discovered this passage in Isaiah. I identified with the "women of Zion," and I agonized with them when I read about God's response to their facade:

> The Lord will smite with a scab the heads of the daughters of
> Zion, and the LORD will lay bare their secret parts. In that day the
> Lord will take away [their] finery.... Instead of perfume there will
> be rottenness; and instead of a girdle, a rope; and instead of well-
> set hair, baldness; and instead of a rich robe, a girding of sackcloth;
> instead of beauty, shame. (Isaiah 3:17-18,24, KJV)

Why, I wondered, did God go to such drastic lengths with these women? God's unveiling of the women of Zion is the deep fear of every woman controlled by perfectionism: *Someday I won't be able to keep it all together, and I will be ugly and alone.*

My heart flinched as I read this passage. What kind of God destroys my facade in order to reveal my imperfections? This question took on deeper meaning and significance to me as I was forced to face my alcoholism and began to confess it to my family and friends. I was right—they were shocked, afraid, sad, and some were angry with me. Survival without alcohol was hard. Living without my facade of "looking good" seemed impossible.

Slowly, however, I was able to look others in the eyes and see compassion and kindness. Perfectionism keeps us from receiving from others, you know. When I was stripped of my "finery," I had no choice but to receive from others or live in isolation.

My counselor said to me, "Sharon, didn't you know that everyone struggles with something? Most people won't hate you for your struggle but will be glad for the opportunity to extend grace to you." I didn't know, because I'd rarely allowed myself to need anything from anyone before. In my hour of need, I discovered the joy of imperfection: authentic relationships and an open door to loving and being loved extravagantly.

But the greatest joy came in discovering why God is committed to revealing our frailties. He promised the women of Zion after he uncovered them: "[I] will be a shelter and shade from the heat of the day, and a refuge and hiding place from the storm and rain" (Isaiah 4:6). God longs to tear away our veil of perfection so that *he* might be our covering!

How grateful I am now for my many imperfections. Without them I would not know unconditional love, forgiveness, and acceptance. Sebastian

Moore writes of this extravagant love in *The Crucified Jesus Is No Stranger:* "Only to your lover do you expose your worst. To an amazed world, Jesus calls for our confession only so that He may reveal Himself in a person's depths as his lover."

Stripping away the facade of appearance allows us to be loved as we are and in turn frees our hearts to love others. When I see weaknesses and mistakes in myself or in others, I no longer have to stiffen in fear and judgment. I can bring failure into the light because I know about forgiveness, and the covering of God's forgiveness allows me to extend to others the grace and love that "covers over a multitude of sins" (1 Peter 4:8).

The Framework of Control

The woman ruled by idealism spends her heart's energy trying to make things as they "ought to be." Her three favorite phrases are *could have, should have,* and *would have.*

When Emily and I eventually discussed with Diane our different responses to her lateness, we laughed at our individual ways of pursuing control. Emily admitted she believed Diane *could have* been on time, *should have* called to say she'd be late, and *would have* been more conscientious if she really cared about our friendship. I believed Emily *could have* let this episode slide, because we *should have* only pleasant times together, and we *would have* good times if everyone would just get along. Neither Emily nor I was wrong in our suppositions, but if we allowed them to control our interactions we might miss something more important in the relationship while insisting on our standards.

The reality is that people are often late with good reason, and Emily's rigid expectations might discourage others from even trying to be her friend. It is also true that sometimes friends are careless and take each other for granted, and my avoidance of the issue might keep the relationship from deepening by using openly discussed mistakes and failures to promote mutual growth and trust in one another. Both Emily's and my idealism had the potential to keep us from being present in the moment, being open to surprise, and from impacting each other in good ways.

When we live with an urgency to take control of people and situations with a demand for "how things ought to be," we cannot be present in the moment. When our life's work is the improvement of others and the world around us, we cannot enjoy what we are in the midst of. Extravagant love involves learning how to live well in the midst of chaos, disappointment, and miscues.

My friend Joan has wonderful ways of inviting me to look and laugh at my own perfectionist tendencies. One night not long ago she surprised me (it's hard to surprise controlling women because we are always anticipating and regulating events around us), pulled me from my home (she didn't even let me comb my hair or change out of my sweats!), and took me to a bingo parlor. I'd never been to a bingo parlor, and I always suspected it might be a den of suburban gambling. I felt disheveled, unprepared for this night of "fun," and wary of Joan's chosen activity.

And—surprise—I had a great time! I laughed as we were on our way out of the bingo hall and saw a sign on the door that read: "You must be present to win." A good lesson for a woman under the influence of idealism! When we are not trying to orchestrate the people and events in our life, we can be more present in each moment, and we might be surprised at how much fun we have.

Idealists are often gifted with sensitivity, intuitiveness, and great vision. But when our hearts are energized to compel others and our environment to fit our expectations, our capacity to impact others positively is limited.

Once after I spoke at a parenting conference, a dear older woman approached me with tears streaming down her face. She described how idealism can poison parenting, and she expressed deep regret for her own unrealistic and idealistic parenting: "I expected my son to be a certain way, no matter what," she explained. "I crushed his individuality and drove him away from me."

Remember the "standoff" in the coffee shop I described earlier in this chapter? We endured about five minutes of awkward conversation before Emily and I confessed to Diane our controlling ideas about how we should spend the rest of our time together. The three of us ended up having a meaningful discussion about Diane's chronic lateness, Emily's judgmental disposition, and my people-pleasing cowardice. Our conversation enriched our friendships and our individual growth because we were able to look at one another and ourselves with eyes of grace. The focus of the conversation for each of us became not "How You Ought to Change," but "How Can I Change?"—how to be a better friend and godly woman.

Discarding the framework of control allows us to build a different framework of presence, openness, and vital give-and-take, which is the lifeblood of healthy relationships. And what a relief to discover that we don't always have to be in charge!

The Foundation of Legalism

Controlling behavior is often founded on a desperation for approval—from others and from God. We long for unconditional love, but our perfectionism keeps us from believing it when it's offered and keeps us working to obtain approval and acceptance on our own merits. The foundation of legalism is a focus on ourselves, which results in lonely, unending striving, aloofness from others, and independence from God.

The apostle Paul wrote an entire epistle warning about the shaky foundation of perfectionism: "I am astonished that you are so quickly deserting the one who called you by the grace of Christ…. Are you so foolish? After beginning with the Spirit, are you now trying to attain your goal by human effort?" (Galatians 1:6; 3:3).

Legalism ignores the truth that we all suffer from the same condition: "For all have sinned and fall short of the glory of God" (Romans 3:23). Imperfection links us. Legalism, on the other hand, encourages a stance of "us against them." The words of the Pharisee in the New Testament are a good example of how wrapping ourselves in perfectionism can keep our hearts aloof from others: "God, I thank you that I am not like other men" (Luke 18:11). Idealists are in danger of becoming persistent critics.

Paradoxically, in imperfection we find not despair but joy, because it compels us to seek help for what we cannot face or accomplish alone. Emily and I could have easily used our individual brands of control to drive a wedge in our relationship. Instead we chose to disclose ourselves to each other, learn from each other, and encourage each other to grow. Our imperfections also highlight our need for God, for Someone to finally come along and put an end to our constant striving.

Shattering the foundation of perfectionism allows us to feel less alone, to depend on others, and ultimately to depend on God. We make room for God as we acknowledge our imperfections. Our imperfections as well as the shortcomings of others bring us face to face with the reality that no matter how hard we try, we are not the ones in control. And this realization brings us closer to the God who is.

I do not understand the mystery of God's meeting us in our need. It happens, of course, at conversion, but I believe God longs to wrap his arms around our neediness over and over again throughout our journey with him. My own need for happiness and harmony, even at the expense of myself or others, so often sends me to God for strength and courage, for grace and forgiveness. I love the words of seventeenth-century poet George Herbert:

And here in dust and dirt, O here,
The lilies of His love appear.

In weakness, strength is discovered. In surrender, peace blossoms.

I once heard a children's pastor explain it this way: God in heaven holds each person by a string. When we fail, we cut the string. Then God ties it up again, making a knot and thereby bringing us a little closer to him. Again and again our failures cut the string, and with each additional knot God keeps drawing us closer and closer.

The apostle Paul writes with joy about a similar discovery: "Now I take limitations in stride, and with good cheer, these limitations that cut me down to size—abuse, accidents, opposition, bad breaks. I just let Christ take over! And so the weaker I get, the stronger I become" (2 Corinthians 12:10, *The Message*).

MY HEART, CHRIST'S HOME

When the Queen of Hearts is banned and we relinquish control, we become free to offer extravagant love. Only when we stop living for control, to get control, to bring others under our control, or to create a perfectly controlled environment do we make room for Christ to indwell us, imperfect as we are.

Nineteenth-century author George MacDonald beautifully describes this intimate indwelling: "A chamber opens up—an inner chamber into which God only can enter." We learn that we are loved unconditionally and accepted, not because of what we do, but because of God's grace and what Christ has done on our behalf. And grace becomes the life force that leads us into extravagant love.

"So what do we do? Keep on sinning so God can keep on forgiving? I should hope not!... [Because you are forgiven,] throw yourselves whole-heartedly and full-time...into God's way of doing things. Sin can't tell you how to live. After all, you're not living under that old tyranny any longer. You're living in the freedom of God" (Romans 6:1,13-14, *The Message*).

The freedom from the tyranny of control allows us to love extravagantly as we experience God's extravagant love for imperfect people.

For example, when my husband was in law school, we were poor. We lived in a three-room apartment in a fourplex at the edge of town. Our carpet was green and soggy near the bathroom due to a shower leak that we couldn't pinpoint or fix. We lived in the muggy South, and mildew grew inside our curtains, behind our refrigerator, and underneath the sink. We cooled the hot, humid summer heat with a window unit that generated more noise than cool air. And if you watched long enough, you could always catch a cockroach scurrying from one part of the kitchen to another.

Near the end of our first year of married life, a lawyer my husband worked for during his undergraduate days called to say he and his wife were coming through town and would like to stop in for dinner. I recalled their beautiful home with plush carpets, soft leather sofas, and air conditioning. I remembered meals in their home that could have been photographed for the pages of *Bon Appetit*.

Dave and I saved every extra penny for three weeks so that we could take this couple to one of the nicer restaurants in town. We planned to meet them at the front door and quickly guide them back to their car and on to the restaurant. But things did not go exactly as we had planned. They arrived, surveyed our home (you could see it all from the front door), and exclaimed, "What a lovely home you have!" Unfazed by the smell of mildew and the warm temperature, they pulled up chairs and motioned for us to sit down as well.

My heart sank as I spied a cockroach scampering across the kitchen linoleum. My eyes pleaded with Dave, "Let's get out of here!"

Dave explained that we'd planned to take them out to dinner and that we'd better get going soon. I'll never forget their response. Our lawyer friend replied, "Oh, we hoped that we could just order pizza. We want to have as much time as possible to hear about your lives and enjoy you in your home."

Enjoy me? In my home—mildew, bugs, green carpet and all? Somehow our little apartment didn't look so shabby in the light of our friends' love for us and desire to be with us.

I have thought of this story often when I consider my heart as Christ's home. He takes up residence *to enjoy me*. Amazing! When I invite him in, the light of his love and desire for me dispels all darkness. And as I rest from striving, allowing him to make himself at home in my heart, I have access to his heart. Once again I learn that loving extravagantly becomes possible only as I am stunned by the knowledge that he loves me first.

Abandoning control reveals our need for a God who comes alongside us, comforts us, sticks with us, and supports us in the realities of life. Understanding my longing for control and perfection leads me to awe and gratitude for a God who not only loves imperfect women, but also longingly invites them to intimacy!

When George MacDonald writes of the place in us where only God can enter, he goes on to write of the place in God where only we can enter, a unique place for each person.

> There is a chamber also (O God, humble and accept my speech),
> a chamber in God Himself, into which none can enter but the
> one, the individual, the peculiar man—out of which chamber that
> man has to bring revelation and strength for his brethren. This is
> that for which he was made—to reveal the secret things of the
> Father.

Oh, the wonder of the give and take of extravagant love!

LIVING IN LOVE

For Personal Reflection and Discussion

1. How and when do you express need, weakness, or struggle?
2. How and when do you withdraw from relationships? Cling to them?
3. Are your expectations in relationships higher than those of other people? Are you able to meet your own standards? Are others able to meet your standards?
4. Respond to the following statements with "True" or "False."

   ___ It is easy for me to accept compliments.

   ___ I am easily offended.

   ___ I am more critical of myself than others.

   ___ I believe it is important to be exceptionally good at something.

__ I spend a lot of time thinking about past mistakes.

__ I am often unaware of what I am feeling.

__ I don't second-guess myself.

__ I dwell on criticism.

__ When I make a mistake, I enjoy the opportunity to learn from it.

__ If I can't do something well, I'd rather not do it.

__ It is easy for me to ask for help.

__ If someone criticizes me or disagrees with me, I assume they don't like me.

__ I believe I could always do better.

5. What do your answers reveal about your own "controlling" tendencies?

Into Action

1. Choose one relationship to evaluate. List in one column your desires for and from this relationship. In another column make notes about the ways you are demanding in this relationship. In the third column begin to list creative alternatives to the demanding behaviors. I've offered one example to get you started.

Desire	Demanding	Creative Alternative
Meaningful conversation	Nagging, pouting	Send an invitation for "a date" for a conversation

2. Ask one or two close friends or family members:

   a. Have you noticed ways in which I have overly high expectations?

    b.   How are you affected by my high standards?

    c.   In what areas would you like to see me relax my expectations?

3. Look for and delight in the "imperfections" of the world around you. For example, in nature take note of how icicles, wind, dust, and "critters" leave things a bit untidy, but beautiful. Where do we get the idea that perfection is attainable or even desirable?

CHAPTER 5

A Heart of Stone

A hardhearted woman. When you hear that description, what pictures come to your mind?

If you had asked me some time ago, I would have described a country music stereotype. I thought a woman with a heart of stone lived a harsh life and was insensitive to the niceties of home, friends, and family. That was until my friend Jane told me her story.

Jane and her family lived in the next block. Her husband, Gordon, was a sales rep for Ford Motor Company. We often teased them about their frequent acquisitions of new cars, and I commiserated with Jane about her husband's long hours and frequent trips away from home.

One year ago, Gordon lost his job. I had no idea what a wild roller coaster this job loss and transition to a new job became for Jane.

"We knew we could live off our savings until Gordon found a new job," she recently explained, "but we also knew we would have to cut out all extras and live very frugally. I didn't tell anyone, even my parents, about our tight financial condition. I didn't want anyone to feel sorry for us, and I thought we'd be just fine."

Before I could express my sorrow for Jane's aloneness in her time of need, she hurried on. "At first we did okay, but then I began to resent not being able to eat out in a restaurant. I noticed the new clothes my friends wore, I envied them, and I literally began to curse the mall every time I drove by.

"And poor Gordon. I nagged him about his job search and constantly reminded him of what we lacked. I turned into a hardhearted woman."

Her description surprised me, and I sympathized, "I think any woman could understand your stress."

"Yes, but my negativity and complaints infected our whole family," she continued. "The boys started feeling sorry for themselves and whining about what everyone else had. I didn't even correct them. Their lament seemed justified.

"I feel so ashamed when I think about that time now. We were going without new clothes, movies, and dinners out, and yet we still had our nice home and two cars and more than many people in the world will ever have.

"The last straw, and turning point, came for me when I wanted a new outfit to wear to a Christmas party. I couldn't believe my luck when I found a beautiful dress at the secondhand store. It fit perfectly and cost less than twenty dollars! All the good feelings about that dress soured, though, when we arrived at the party. I couldn't help but compare it to the newer styles everyone else was wearing. I felt mad at Gordon all over again, and I ignored the bewildered look on his face when he sensed my anger.

"And then you won't believe what happened! I bumped into a woman I had met at last year's party. These were her exact words: 'That dress looks lovely on you. Maybe you remember that I wore that same dress last year.'

"I didn't even respond. I grabbed Gordon's arm and told him I couldn't stay a minute longer. We rode home in silence, and I stormed up to my room to throw a major pity party! I tore off my secondhand dress and threw myself across my bed.

"But before I could begin to rehearse my woes, a verse from Scripture popped into my head. I couldn't get it out of my mind, and before long it made its way into my heart: 'It is better to live in a corner of a roof than in a house shared with a contentious woman' (Proverbs 21:9, NASB). Slowly, my heart began to soften as I saw and confessed my ungrateful heart."

Jane went on to tell me about learning to be thankful and discovering the radical difference it made in the life of their family during that difficult time. I left that conversation with Jane with a new picture of a hardhearted woman and with a determination to reexamine my own life.

Remember that the energy of the heart involves brain and emotion, thought and passion, vision and feeling. Quoting Isaiah, Jesus explains in the Gospels what happens when we refuse to see and understand our own hearts: "Their eyes are blinded, their hearts are hardened, so that they wouldn't see with their eyes and perceive with their hearts, and turn to me, God, so I could heal them" (John 12:40, *The Message*). A refusal to recognize our unthankful heart and acknowledge its impact on our relationships results in living with a heart of stone—a heart that is lifeless and ineffective in relationships.

A stony, ungrateful spirit is born in and nursed by four uniquely feminine behaviors in relationships: jealousy, comparisons, envy, and gossip.

JEALOUSY

Understanding jealousy, a natural, recurrent emotion in our relationships, is essential in keeping our hearts free for extravagant love. Jealousy, unchecked, inevitably results in comparisons, envy, and gossip, carrying away captive all our heart energy.

My friend, Laura, told me about her encounter with jealousy at church, of all places! "I didn't even stay for the church service," Laura admitted. "I know it's petty and immature, but I don't ever want to go to Sunday school again!"

Laura explained that she had introduced two of her friends to each other, and they had become fast friends. At first, she congratulated herself on bringing the two together, but lately she had started to regret her initiative. She suspected the two new friends liked each other more than they liked her, and when she watched them leave the Sunday school class together without waiting for her, she felt hurt, left out, embarrassed, and a little angry.

She left Sunday school and decided to skip church completely that day. One of the friends called her later to ask why she wasn't in church and told her they had saved a place for her. Although the call soothed Laura's hurt, she still felt that these friendships were slipping away from her and she should probably concentrate on other relationships and just let these go. Laura concluded, "My mom always said, 'Three girls can never be friends,' and I'm starting to believe her!"

Laura's story is a familiar example of jealousy—that sapping, sinking sense of being left out, deprived, abandoned, forgotten, passed over. *Webster's Dictionary* defines it this way: "apprehension of being displaced, fear of being supplanted in affection; distrust of the fidelity of a beloved person."

But are such feelings all bad? While we fear that jealousy reveals insecurity, instability, and immaturity, and can even lead to murderous behavior, the truth is that jealousy is another imprint of God's design on our hearts.

Consider God's words about his own jealous heart: "Do not worship any other god, for the LORD, whose name is Jealous, is a jealous God" (Exodus 34:14). Just as God's jealousy reveals amazing aspects of his character and his extravagant heart for us, jealousy has the potential to reveal wonderful attributes in us.

The roots of jealousy are clearly exposed in Laura's story and Webster's definition. Jealousy grows out of a longing to be considered, remembered, included. Jealousy is cultivated by a desire for permanence, security, and abiding relationships. Jealousy is vulnerable to loss, winces at betrayal, and hates unfaithfulness. The roots of jealousy reveal the holy longing for relationships that God has written in our hearts.

In Laura's case, however, her legitimate longing for good things with her friends quickly turned to suspicion, anger, and withdrawal from relationships. I wondered if things might have turned out differently if she could have identified the sinking feeling when she watched her friends leave the Sunday school class without her, expressed her fears and concerns to her friends, and remained a part of the threesome.

But jealousy makes us feel too vulnerable. We don't want to appear overly sensitive or needy. We'd rather gather up our pride, retreat from relationships, and nurse our wounds in private. Admit to being jealous? No way!

God, on the other hand, not only admits to being jealous, he goes so far as to say, "[My] name is Jealous." God so longs for faithful, intimate, abiding relationships with us that he is not ashamed to express his fear of losing us, his desire for unending relationship, and his hurt from and hatred of unfaithfulness. God embraces his holy jealousy to assure us of his love, to remind us to remain faithful, and to encourage us that he will never leave us or forsake us. God risks being passed over in favor of others and being humiliated by betrayal.

Why would the God of the universe take such risks and open himself up to the pain and humiliation of jealousy? For the chance of a relationship with us and to model to us how to engage in extravagant relationships. I marvel at the words: "'He throws caution to the winds, giving to the needy in reckless abandon. His right-living, right-giving ways never run out, never wear out. This most generous God…is more than extravagant with you. He gives you something you can then give away, which grows into full-formed lives, robust in God, wealthy in every way, so that you can be generous in every way, producing with us great praise to God" (2 Corinthians 9:9-11, *The Message*).

Identifying jealousy, and the holy longing at its root, can allow us to disclose our hearts to our loved ones and to stay deeply connected in relationships. Identifying jealousy can also enable us to examine our relationships and evaluate the most prudent course. When we understand our own jealousy, we are able to set boundaries and expose destructive patterns in relationships.

A couple who came to see me for marriage counseling expressed concern about their inability to trust each other. The wife explained that she thought the problem was her insecurity and awkwardness in social situations. She often felt left out and disregarded by her husband.

When I suggested that her longing for security and a sense of belonging and her desire to feel special to her husband were all good expressions of what she was made for, she was able to look at their relationship through a lens of self-respect instead of self-contempt. We discussed the fact that her husband would often engage in conversations with others so intently that he left his wife out completely. She admitted that she felt forgotten and jealous. Her husband recognized how he inadvertently provoked her jealousy.

The simple identification and admission of jealousy allowed this couple to not only deepen trust in their relationship but to discuss ways to grow together as a couple. The wife committed to signaling her husband when she felt left out by touching his elbow, and he agreed to work on consciously including her in his conversations.

Unfortunately, we seldom use jealousy in productive and life-giving ways. It seems too risky to reveal our hearts and trust others. Our hearts are not free for the risk-taking, recklessly abandoned, steadfastly extravagant love modeled by the God whose name is Jealous because all too often our jealousy leads us to behaviors that harden our hearts and impoverish our relationships.

As I write this afternoon, trying to sort out the "godly jealousy" Paul talks about in 2 Corinthians 11:2 from the petty, withering jealousy I know we've all experienced, I am looking at a climbing vine on the side of our fence. It is almost impossible to follow an individual vine with the eye, to keep it separate from the dozens of others that twist and turn back in upon themselves. Untangling jealousy will require that we look at different strands that grow from its root, strands that often strangle the life out of our passion for relationships, resulting in a hard, ungrateful heart. These are the strands of comparison, envy, and gossip.

Perhaps you, like me, wince at confronting these "feminine wiles" that all too often sour our lives and the lives of those around us. But I am convinced that when we understand ourselves and bring the whole truth about ourselves to God, we are no longer propelled by forces that we are too afraid or ashamed to expose to the light. We no longer live lives of discontent and misery because we will not name the emotions and activities that infect our lives. We no longer have hearts of stone incapable of pumping life into our relationships. Rather, we have hearts of flesh that are wholeheartedly engaged in extravagant relationships. This is the promise God gave to the prophet Ezekiel: "I will remove from you your heart of stone and give you a heart of flesh.... I will put breath in you, and you will come to life" (Ezekiel 36:26; 37:6).

COMPARISONS

Jealousy that is not recognized and directed toward positively impacting relationships quickly turns to comparisons, draining the heart of gratitude. We compare our shoes, bodies, children, cars, housecleaning skills, jobs, vacations—even the whiteness of our teeth! Comparison distorts our longing to belong and our fear of loss into a competition in which we believe that whoever has the most and the best wins.

Comparisons involve quantifying and measuring one thing against another, an activity that has to do with the "material." The danger of comparison is that it locks us into the material. Comparisons seduce us into wanting more and more and never enjoying what we already have. That's why Scripture exhorts: "When they measure themselves by themselves and compare themselves with themselves, they are not wise" (2 Corinthians 10:12), and reminds us: "So we fix our eyes not on what is seen, but on what is unseen. For what is seen is temporary, but what is unseen is eternal" (2 Corinthians 4:18).

Not only do comparisons keep us occupied with superficial concerns, but they diminish our capacity for relationships. We may think we are being humble when we say, "I'm just not as talented as she is. I can't sing or speak or relate to people like others can." This false humility, however, only keeps us from identifying and expressing our unique giftedness. True humility does not make comparisons, but identifies, gives thanks for, and uses the talents and abilities God has uniquely bestowed upon us.

Comparisons also ultimately produce a biting, spiteful spirit. Perhaps the most difficult verse in the Bible to live out fully and authentically is Romans 12:15: "Rejoice with those who rejoice and weep with those who weep" (NASB). When we compare ourselves, we cannot live in accordance with this scripture. In simpler and sadder terms, when we are ruled by comparison, it is almost easier to admire a stranger than our best friend.

One woman I know caught herself in the ugly trap of comparisons. She lamented: "It seems that all my friends are getting married. I don't think I can stand to buy another wedding present. I know I'm supposed to be happy for them and satisfied with God since he's probably the only man I'll ever have in my life!"

She stopped short after this sentence, surprised by her own sarcastic meanness. Comparisons use our heart's energy for superficial concerns and blind us to our own gifts and talents, resulting in a stony heart that makes us come across as petty, ungracious, and unkind.

Comparisons keep us from developing a healthy self-image and keep us focused on what we don't have. Contrary to what we often believe, self-esteem is not something that is given to us or that results from favorable life circumstances—and that is really good news. Self-esteem is something we give to ourselves. The discipline of developing the muscles of self-esteem is like the discipline of any other exercise.

At least once a year I decide to start jogging (again). The first few days of the exercise seem pointless, awkward, and hard. But as I persist, the movements take on meaning, become more fluid, and are rewarding. The exercises of self-esteem may seem awkward or even ridiculous at first, but they will be worthwhile, and they will keep you from comparing yourself with others and restore your heart to its full capacity for relationships.

The best way to develop your self-esteem and keep from comparing yourself to others is to take inventory. What are your talents, strengths, eccentricities, resources, and passions? One idea I love is when you are looking at magazines, reading the church bulletin, or visiting with friends, begin to tear out pictures, clip quotations, and write down thoughts about what you like, what "feels like you," what stirs your heart, and what you'd like to pursue. This can include everything from decorating schemes to theological concepts. Put your pictures, quotations, and ideas in a notebook or make a collage to hang on a wall. Your notebook or collage will be a constant reminder about the landscape of your unique heart.

One friend of mine began such a notebook and quickly noticed an elegant beauty in all the pictures she collected. She knew that there was something about the word "elegant" that resonated in her heart. As she began to think of herself as an elegant woman, her posture, appearance, and interactions with her husband subtly changed. She stopped nagging. She laid a single rose on her husband's side of the bed with a love note. Whenever she was tempted to spiral into shame about herself, instead of binging on Chee-tos she made a cup of tea and meditated on Psalm 139 or read through her notebook.

Developing self-esteem is work, but it is energy far better spent than being consumed by comparing ourselves to others and ending up with a healthy dose of self-contempt as well as a disgruntled heart toward those around us. So instead of looking for what others have and you don't, begin looking for your positive qualities. This list is the beginning of a portrait of your heart, a picture you will need to look at often to remind yourself that you do have the resources to be an extravagant lover. God created each of us with a unique personality, distinct gifts, and even quirky characteristics to enable us to distinctly and unconventionally love the people around us.

As for our weaknesses, sins, or deficiencies? We must bravely acknowledge these as well. They are part of who we are. Comparisons and the often-accompanying false humility, however, downplay our positives and magnify our negatives. Examining and confessing our failures in the context of forgiveness opens our heart to our inestimable worth in God's eyes and to the reality of extravagant love. Our worth is not determined on the basis of our assets and liabilities. Somebody has already paid the price for us, and that determines our ultimate worth. So we can stop comparing ourselves with others and evaluate ourselves honorably when we grasp God's heart for us, when we dare to start looking at ourselves with the same tenderness, delight, and compassion that he does.

Envy

When I started confronting my own unthankful spirit and examining its roots, I never imagined that an important lesson on this subject would come in my son's fifth-grade classroom. Graham is eleven years old, and he is in life for the fun of it! Staying on task for schoolwork requires constant vigilance and a sense of humor for both of us.

As the end of the school year approached, I started to breathe a sigh of relief that maybe "we" were going to make it past the fifth grade! The last major assignment was a geography project that required extra reading, a report, and a mobile. Graham's country was Norway, and we worked for hours on the project. I went to school with Graham to turn in the project and spend the morning in his classroom for a "World's Fair." All the parents had an opportunity to walk around the room and look at the students' presentations on many different countries.

Graham's display on Norway was next to a display on Germany. I tried not to compare "our" handiwork of yarn, cutout pictures, and neatly labeled points-of-interest to the project on Germany. The Germany display looked professionally engineered with computer-generated graphics and perfectly balanced pictures. I quickly consoled myself that Germany is a much easier country to learn about and report on than Norway, but I sensed growing resentment for whoever was responsible for the Germany display. For a moment I forgot all the fun Graham and I had working on this project. Just hours before, we had laughed at his lopsided pictures and congratulated ourselves on finding so many interesting facts about such an obscure country. Jealousy took a dark turn in my heart as I compared the projects, and I even considered complaining to the teacher about the inequities in assignments.

And then Graham introduced me to Jeremy, the proud builder of the Germany project. I had met Jeremy before and knew he was a great kid, but very different from Graham—straight-A student, neatly organized, never lost a paper. Jeremy's mother approached us, and I was considering not liking her for no other reason than the notion that her son was "better" than mine.

When jealousy goes unchecked and we begin to make comparisons, the inevitable progression is to envy. *Webster's Dictionary* defines *envy* this way: "to feel displeasure and ill-will at the superiority of another in happiness, success, reputation, or the possession of anything desirable; vexed or discontent at the good fortune or qualities of another." If jealousy fears to lose what it has, envy is pained at seeing another have what it wants for itself.

Mothers everywhere know that nothing stirs longings within us like our children. We long for them to be happy, successful, and good. And when our children struggle due to their unique makeup or their bad choices, we hurt. When I compared Graham to Jeremy, I ached for my son and his struggles academically (not to mention his lopsided display). I allowed the misery of envy to invade my heart. I resented Jeremy's mother for having a son who didn't struggle as mine did.

Does it surprise you that something as simple as a fifth-grade geography project could produce such crazy thinking? I invite you to examine your own thoughts when jealousy goes unchecked and is allowed free rein.

Jeremy's mother greeted me sweetly, looked at the displays, and announced, "We are so proud of Jeremy. He has worked hard and has gotten straight A's all year long." As Graham's last report card flashed before my eyes, I winced at the C's—and I decided I did not like Jeremy's mom one bit!

An envious woman sickens at the sight of other people's success. I replied defensively, "We've been traveling a lot this year speaking for Family-Life, and so school has not always been our priority." I hated the feelings gripping my heart and thought the only way to stop them was to put Jeremy's mother in her place by highlighting my own achievements. Envy is only at ease in the misery of others.

Jeremy's mother would have been flabbergasted at the machinations of my heart. She replied kindly and with curiosity, "I didn't know you spoke for FamilyLife." However, since I had already made her an enemy in my mind, I perceived her response as one of mockery and accusation. In my heart, infected by comparison and envy, I heard her say, "I didn't know *you* (you, with the messy, late, C-student son) spoke for a respected organization." All endeavors to satisfy an envious woman are fruitless, because envy cultivates dissatisfaction, suspicion, and distrust.

I called three friends when I got home to tell them about the horrific encounter with Jeremy's mom. And you can bet that I did not portray her in a favorable light. Instead, I quickly proceeded to the next step in jealousy's dark progression: gossip.

Envy wallows in wishes and fantasies of things being different than the way they are. Envy ultimately wants to eliminate the object of envy. Envy destroys what it most admires and cannot have for itself. Ah yes, envy can turn an ordinary mom into a hardhearted killer.

GOSSIP

Murder. Yes, that is a good synonym for gossip. Gossip is the wounding or killing of another's reputation. The apostle James writes a poignant description of the violence of envy: "You want something but don't get it. You kill and covet, but you cannot have what you want" (James 4:2).

Gossip feels powerful. It is a dark way to gain a sense of control by crushing another's reputation with words. Although my friends did not know Jeremy's mom, although I wasn't saying anything that wasn't true, and although I was just "sharing" about my day, I knew that I was talking about someone in a way in which I would not speak of them in their presence—and that's gossip.

Gossip shows up repeatedly in Scripture's lists of heinous sins (with adultery, murder, and theft) because it kills the heart of another human being. Gossip breaks confidentiality (Proverbs 11:13), causes division, and sets one person against another (16:28). It felt good to tell my friends about Jeremy's mom and receive their empathy for me in return. Gossip creates a false sense of intimacy.

Proverbs describes the delectable feeling gossips creates, for a moment: "The words of a gossip are like choice morsels; they go down to a [woman's] inmost parts" (26:22). However, the apostle Paul warns that a woman cannot be considered trustworthy if she gossips, which means she won't be fulfilled in any of her relationships (1 Timothy 3:11). Gossip steals the energy of the heart. It takes thought, emotion, planning, and passion to gossip.

I hung up the telephone from the gossip sessions with my friends and plopped down at the kitchen table. My heart felt as heavy as lead, and I knew that the energy of my heart was almost totally depleted after spending a few hours controlled by comparison, envy, and gossip. I knew the possibility of loving extravagantly was completely jeopardized by the dark and destructive forces that had carried away my heart captive. I prayed, "God, help me."

Gratitude

Guilt can be such a blessing. Just as a pain in the body may be a warning of physical injury or sickness, guilt is an ache in the soul that often signals us to examine our hearts for sin. If we can admit we engage in comparisons, envy, and gossip, we can say we are sorry and work on avoiding those behaviors in the future. The wonder of knowing our own hearts is that we can confess our sins, and God "is faithful and just and will forgive us our sins and purify us from all unrighteousness" (1 John 1:9).

I glanced at a picture of Graham on our refrigerator. I smiled at his exuberance and sparkling eyes. How I love him! He keeps us laughing and is never lacking for words. Suddenly I felt gratitude, the antidote for my hardened heart.

Gratitude moves us from believing we are lacking to rejoicing that we are blessed. Gratitude is the difference between thank you and gimme, between admiration and envy, between wonder and misery. Gratitude diminishes envy until we are truly glad for the good fortune of others. *Webster's Dictionary* defines *gratitude* like this: "warm and friendly feeling toward a benefactor, conscious of benefits received and kindly disposed toward benefactor." Gratitude frees us to rejoice with those who rejoice. We become generous of spirit. We can be extravagant lovers.

As I confessed my sin and thanked God for my wonderful son, I saw the events in the classroom with clearer eyes. I saw that I was the one worried that Graham wasn't doing well enough in school, that I was the one who was insecure about the lopsided geography project, and that I was holding Jeremy's mother responsible for my own negative interpretation of her words.

Of course, it would have done her little good for me to confess all the strange twists and turns of my heart. I decided instead that my repentance would be to bake some chocolate chip cookies and deliver them with a kind note. I don't bake very often, but my heart sang as I measured flour and mixed ingredients.

When I picked up Graham from school the next afternoon, he announced, "Guess what, Mom! I got an A- on the geography project!" I had the fleeting thought that Jeremy probably got an A+, but the smile on Graham's face quickly reminded me to be grateful.

The reason we are sometimes impoverished in spirit is not because of what we lack, but because we really don't have much if we are not grateful. Gratitude is a posture of the heart. Posture is what makes certain activities possible. When I stand, I can walk or run. When I sit, I can lean back and relax. When I kneel, I can pray. When I lie down, I can rest or sleep. When I am grateful, I can receive. Identifying the inevitable human emotion of jealousy reminds me to assume a posture that prepares me to receive. It may seem crazy that at the very moment of feared loss I should prepare for blessing, but that is the path to extravagant love.

Comparison, envy, and gossip can absorb all our heart's energy, turning it into a heart of stone and resulting in a narrow, pinched life. Gratitude breathes life into our hearts for relationships. Cultivating gratitude is an art and a discipline that is possible as we develop healthy self-esteem, view the people in our lives as gifts to teach and help transform us into the image of

God, and continue to meditate on God's love for us. "Moved by the extravagance of God...[we'll] respond.... Thank God for this gift, his gift. No
language can praise it enough!" (2 Corinthians 9:12-13,15, *The Message*).

LIVING IN LOVE

For Personal Reflection and Discussion

1. What is your response when you feel left out, deprived, forgotten,
   or passed over?

2. How do you regard self-esteem?

unimportant	a natural occurrence
something to work on	the same as self-centeredness
a valuable commodity	beside the point

3. Can you recall a time when someone rejoiced with you? Describe
   the impact their rejoicing had on you.

4. What do you believe is most important about yourself: intelligence, achievements, relationships, appearance?

Into Action

1. Monitor your self-esteem over the next two weeks. If you notice it
   sagging, write down what happened that day. What triggered the
   low evaluation of yourself? Ask yourself three questions:

   a. How would I interpret this event if it happened to someone
      else?

   b. What positive action can I take?

   c. How can I handle the situation if it happens again?

2. For the next week, don't go to sleep without expressing gratitude to another person and to God. Do you notice a difference in your outlook on life?

3. Read the book of Deuteronomy and look for evidence of God's jealousy.

CHAPTER 6

Affairs of the Heart

Few books have captured the hearts and imaginations of women like Robert James Waller's novel *The Bridges of Madison County*. I've been surprised by the number of women who saw themselves in the story of Francesca, the Iowa farm wife who became entangled in an affair with Robert Kincaid, the traveling photographer who showed up on her doorstep. Women are drawn to the promise of romance, two-hanky movies, and love affairs of the rich and famous—to stories that ignite something in our hearts. And then we wipe our tears, close the book, and shake our heads in dismay while we get busy fixing dinner.

What spark is ignited by stories, songs, and movies about loving and being loved? It is a connection with what we were made for. I'm not talking about an adulterous fling with a fantasy paramour, but instead our God-given desire for passionate, real relationships with husband, friends, children, parents, neighbors, coworkers, grandchildren—and God.

Remember, the holy longing for meaningful relationships is written into our hearts by our Creator. It whispers to us, nudges us toward relationships, and reminds us of the joy found when we are truly engaged in relationship. But when our innate longings are ignored, discounted, disappointed, misunderstood, or disregarded, our hearts often search for some satisfaction through unhealthy means. Rather than consciously pursuing righteous relationships and a meaningful life of love, we allow poor substitutes to capture our hearts.

We seldom leap into affairs of the heart. Most often such affairs are subtle, gradual relationships that develop as a result of the choices we make about where we will spend our passion. We can have affairs of the heart with food, shopping, sexual fantasy, being liked, helping others, work, gambling, alcohol, drugs—the list is endless. There are an infinite number of ways to avoid the deepest feelings and longings of the heart. Proverbs 19:21 says, "There are many devices in a [woman's] heart" (KJV).

An affair of the heart is any relationship, behavior, or experience that supplants healthy relationships and replaces God as central in our lives. The prophet Isaiah describes the adulterous heart: "These people come near to me with their mouth and honor me with their lips, but their hearts are far from me" (Isaiah 29:13).

Affairs of the heart take root when we discover a relationship that initially promises to be safe, satisfying, predictable, and within our control. Affairs of the heart grow as we relinquish not only our longings but also our will to these negative relationships. We become willing to sacrifice time, judgment, healthy relationships, even our spiritual life to the overtly destructive or subtly deadening relationship substitute. Affairs of the heart flourish as we surrender our God-given desires to people, behaviors, or things that eventually rule our lives.

KIDNAPPED HEARTS

The woman who habitually runs to the cookie jar when life is unsettling is no different from the woman who turns to soap operas for an hour-long respite from her own life. The woman who soothes her longing for relationship by running herself ragged at work is a lot like the woman who satiates her longings with promiscuous relationships. Although the external realities may look different, the internal state of the heart is the same—captured and carried away by a "relationship" that robs the heart of the energy necessary to live a life of extravagant love and passionate purpose.

I can picture the faces of countless women I know who found themselves "captured and carried away" by choices that kidnapped their hearts and diverted their passion:

- The Bible study leader whose eyes are lined with fatigue and whose heart is filled with frenzy…and still she cannot say no.
- The office administrator who goes home after work and eats a whole bag of potato chips, hates herself, and feels inferior to others.
- The middle-class mom with the minivan and the secret stash of marijuana in her bedroom closet.
- The mother of two preschoolers whose lonely, hectic hours include a madness that she does not dare admit—soap operas, romance novels, and habitual sexual fantasy.
- The busy woman who doesn't have time for friends.
- The deacon's wife with the flawless makeup who doesn't know how to begin to confess her obsession with her appearance and the toll it is taking on her soul.
- The hard-working saleswoman who spends almost every dime she makes for things she doesn't need and puts her family in peril because they don't have money for things they do need.

My own affair of the heart was with alcohol. Even though I was a Christian woman who cared deeply about God and my family, I fell in love with alcohol because it initially offered me a safe and satisfying haven.

Shortly after I was married in my twenties, I began experiencing what I now know were panic attacks. The tensions of marriage, the loneliness of living two thousand miles away from family and friends, and my intense perfectionist personality combined to produce a roller coaster of emotions that I was not equipped to handle and a thirst that I was desperate to quench.

A well-meaning doctor prescribed a glass of wine to soothe my mounting internal tension. Alcohol had never been a part of my life, but I was desperate for some relief from the pain, loneliness, and tension. I did not know any family history that suggested alcohol should be avoided, so I eagerly complied with my doctor's suggestion.

Immediately, I experienced the benefits of alcohol—the temporary satiation of my thirst. It erased tension, eased my loneliness, and relaxed my uptight tendencies. The habitual glass of wine turned into a compulsion that stealthily crept into my daily life. I would hear of friends and family experiencing difficulties and think: "If only they knew about my secret friend. It is always available to make everything better."

But an affair of the heart makes everything better only until it makes everything worse. My love affair with alcohol began to affect my health physically, emotionally, and spiritually. I started needing alcohol to feel normal. I wanted alcohol more than I wanted anything else. And I was consumed with guilt about my growing dependency.

I wasn't sure why alcohol affected me so dramatically. I didn't know who to talk to about it, and I didn't know how to find help. I reached a point where my days were consumed with a desperation to drink and a desperation to stop drinking. I needed help to reclaim the holy thirst of my heart and to refocus on Living Water.

Help and hope began when I told someone the truth. I made an appointment with a Christian counselor, and as I sat with a racing heart in the waiting room, a collage of incongruous images flashed through my mind: trash cans crammed with vodka bottles, Christmas tins packed for the elderly, lubricated arguments laced with hateful words that could never be taken back, Sunday school lessons faithfully prepared and articulately delivered, years of anesthetized pain and pleasure, regular attendance at all church functions. I saw the reflection of a life splashed with booze and immersed in the church.

I didn't know then that this shame-filled secret struggle would teach me much about my own heart and God's heart for me. I had no idea that the small, drastic step of telling someone about my relationship with alcohol would begin to infuse my life with meaning and compel me to deepen and enrich my relationships with others and my walk with God. I just knew I couldn't keep my "affair of the heart" secret any longer.

THE STATE OF YOUR HEART

What about you? How can you know if you're involved in an affair of the heart? Destructive relationships are marked by four distinctives: they are *habitual, compulsive, secretive,* and *isolating.* Not all four elements need to be present at the same time, but all will be experienced at some point during the course of the relationship. And all four elements erode a woman's capacity to love and be loved in soul-enriching ways.

Unhealthy Habits

Affairs of the heart result from repeated choices and from learned behavior reinforced by the benefits that it delivers.

Linda struggles with an unhealthy relationship with food. She remembers that this destructive relationship began when she received her driver's license at age sixteen and got permission to drive by herself. Linda's first stop was the 7-Eleven convenience store where she bought a Hostess cherry pie and quickly ate it in the solitude of her car. In contrast to Linda's family problems and academic struggles, this private relationship with food was pleasant and completely under her control.

From that day on, every time stress or loneliness crept into her world, Linda escaped into a world that revolved around the immediate gratification and companionship of food. She mistook her longing to be loved for the longing for cherry pies. Her relationship with food has become increasingly complex, but it began with a sense that she had found a relationship that worked. Now when Linda needs a respite, she doesn't even think about what she will choose. Her retreat to a relationship with food is a habit. "The wonderful thing about food," she says, "is that it won't leave me, hurt me, or talk back to me."

When Linda tries to stay away from food in the midst of emotional turmoil, she feels increased stress—uneasiness, irritability, even mounting panic. She then concludes that the only way to deal with the increased tension is to again retreat to her familiar relationship with food. Her habitual behavior traps her.

The apostle Paul describes the affair of the heart in Ephesians 4:19, "Having lost all sensitivity, they have given themselves over to…[indulgence], with a continual lust for more." The relationship with food, alcohol, spending, performing—whatever one does or uses—is never quite enough. You become accustomed to the benefits of the relationship, which in turn results in an increased craving. You need more and more of the negative behavior to achieve the desired effect. You are always after that comfort and pleasure, always mindful that it's available, always so glad to come back to it, and always committed to never losing it.

But Linda's relationship with food leaves her feeling awful about herself, which in turn keeps her at a distance from others. Her habitual retreat to food closes her heart to other avenues of nourishment, nurture, connection, and companionship.

Compulsive Behavior

Many sincere Christian women regret their sinful and destructive behaviors, express a desire to stop, and yet still end up back in the harmful relationship, seemingly unable to control themselves. Linda told me about walking into a grocery store, buying a dozen doughnuts without thinking about it, and eating half of them before she even got home. She expressed her compulsivity this way: "It's like I hit a blank spot in my brain. I don't think about anything—my kids, my friends, God—I can't help it."

When we feel as if we have no choice, it is typically because we are torn by mixed motives. Linda longs to be free from her enslaving relationship with food, but she also does not want to give it up. Even when a woman knows she's in a destructive relationship, she still desperately desires the satisfaction and control the relationship initially promised.

Compulsion is the act of wrapping ourselves around a substance, a person, or an activity that we believe is capable of taking our despair away, if only temporarily. The obsessive relationship becomes a safe place into which we can pour all our feelings of disappointment, rage, longing, hope, and sorrow. As long as we are obsessed with food, sex, activity, or any other external focus, we always have a concrete reason to explain our emotions.

Giving up a compulsive relationship brings us face to face with the inevitable pain in our lives. No matter how good our lives, we are all subject to loneliness and unfulfilled longings in relationships. When we habitually choose to deny and deaden our longings, we lose the ability to be open to the uncontrollable and unpredictable joy of legitimate relationships.

Rather than experience a pain and joy that are out of our control, many of us choose the misery and shame of a destructive relationship that seems within our control. For Linda, that relationship was with the food she pursued, consumed, and controlled.

Secret Satisfaction

Affairs of the heart are cultivated in a private world of desire and personal choices that provide a sense of relief and control. How can you begin to explain your affair of the heart when you may have never put it into words yourself?

- When I eat "comfort food," I feel less alone.
- After I've had a couple of glasses of wine, life seems more bearable.
- When I buy a new outfit, I feel better about myself.
- If I organize all of my closets, I will feel more in control.
- I deserve the escape of a good romance novel.
- Long, productive hours at work compensate for the struggles and problems in my personal life.
- As long as he/she approves of me, I am okay.

Somewhere, deep inside, you may be aware that you have an unhealthy relationship with food, shopping, drugs, sex, work, or another person, but you fear that no one else can understand your dependency. On one hand you fear you will lose your family, friends, and reputation if you admit to your struggle, and on the other hand you are shaken at the prospect of having to give up your secretly satisfying relationship. Maybe it still "works" for you, and you're not convinced that anything else will. As a result, part of you lives in a private world, alienated from your own heart and isolated from others because you can't let them know about your struggle.

Isolating Choices

No matter how hard you may work to keep your affair of the heart private, such affairs are never completely an individual matter. An affair of the heart gradually kidnaps the whole heart until it is diminished in its capacity to love. Because the energy of your heart is consumed with the unhealthy relationship and with keeping it secret or immune to the positive influence of others, it is not possible to be fully present for yourself, friends, family, coworkers, or God. As a result, you may find yourself increasingly isolated from others.

Linda confessed to me that she often declines invitations from family and friends so she can instead eat in the privacy of her own home. And with profound discouragement, she admits that she cannot freely pray or participate in her church's worship service because of her overwhelming guilt.

BRAVEHEARTS

Affairs of the heart spring from the tension between the desire for relationships and the inevitable uncertainty and disappointments that relationships bring. The good news is that we *all* struggle with surrendering our hearts to gods other than the true and living God. Gerald May in his wonderful book *Addiction and Grace* writes: "The severely addicted people have played out, on an extreme scale, a drama that all human beings experience more subtly and more covertly."

Perhaps examining the four attributes of affairs of the heart has revealed to you a substance, behavior, or person that you believed promised relief from disappointment, but in choosing that relationship repeatedly it has become compulsive, private, and enslaving. You cannot rid yourself of the longing for connection, but you can choose to take your longing to God or to turn away from him. Turning toward him means confessing you are holding onto a destructive relationship and asking for the strength to relax your grip.

Letting go of an affair of the heart requires that you seek out others and develop authentic relationships, compels you to risk that God is good and can be trusted, and restores your self-respect. You will be free to love out of a whole heart and reach for the choices, experiences, and relationships that will fill your life with purpose, integrity, compassion, faith, and hope.

An affair of the heart keeps you from obeying the greatest commandments: "Jesus said, 'Love the Lord your God with all your passion and prayer and intelligence.… Love others as well as you love yourself.' These two commands are pegs; everything in God's Law and the Prophets hangs from them" (Matthew 22:37-40, *The Message*).

In the next chapter you will find three stories of women whose hearts are divided by perfectionism, envy, and addiction. You will recognize the Queen of Hearts, the stony-hearted woman, and the woman whose heart is kidnapped by something other than extravagant love. You will read about their courageous acknowledgment of their captive hearts and their powerful journeys toward becoming women with brave hearts. If you met them, they would appear to be normal Christian women. But they were trapped in patterns of living that stole, undermined, and even destroyed the life that God intends for them to experience.

Today, however, they are women with *great* lives. I have their pictures on a shelf where I can see them often, along with those of many other bravehearts I know. As I look at their pictures, I am reminded that it is possible to be broken and whole at the same time; to rest in deep faith even in the midst of life's storms; to live with fervent hope when apathy or even despair seems more reasonable; and to love radically, thereby redeeming relationships in extravagant ways.

Women with brave hearts know that the greatest life is not necessarily a life in which they marry the man of their dreams, live in a beautiful home in the suburbs, or raise children who never give them a moment's worry or concern. The greatest life does not consist of popularity or prosperity. The greatest life is not realized when we lose ten pounds or get the right haircut and a flattering wardrobe.

The apostle Paul penned the courageous motto of a braveheart: "So, no matter what I say, what I believe, and what I do, I'm bankrupt without love.... We have three things to do...: Trust steadily in God, hope unswervingly, love extravagantly. And the best of the three is love" (1 Corinthians 13:3,13, *The Message*).

I hope that as you read the stories of bravehearts that follow, you will find not only similarities with your own story but also inspiration to follow God with deeper faith. May you be encouraged to hope and dream in new ways, fight complacency, risk more, create wildly, pray fervently, and make good relationships extravagant because you embrace the truth that the greatest life is a life of love.

LIVING IN LOVE

For Personal Reflection and Discussion

1. Do you need to acknowledge a destructive relationship that has you in bondage?
2. When have you made excuses or rationalized to justify destructive behaviors?
3. When have you found yourself caught up in an activity that you would never choose if you had taken time to think about it? How did you get trapped by that activity?

4. On what occasions have you felt you must hide your behavior from others? Be specific about the behavior and why you felt hiding it was essential.

5. How do you feel if you must give up, even temporarily, a certain behavior or relationship?

6. In a typical week, how much time, planning, energy, and worry do you spend in trying to hold on to a destructive activity or relationship?

Into Action

1. Finish these sentences:

    When life is unsettling, I cling to _____.

    When I am upset, I crave _____.

    When I am overwhelmed, I grasp for _____.

    When I am alone, I hold on to _____.

    When I am angry, I want _____.

    When I celebrate, I _____.

    When I am disappointed, I try to _____.

    When I need comfort, I soothe myself by _____.

    If you have difficulty completing these sentences, begin to watch for these emotions: restlessness, pain, loneliness, frustration, anger, joy, disappointment, and note how you respond or if you numb, dismiss, or deny the emotions. This exercise can give you clues about the "devices" of your heart.

2. Experiment with eliminating a negative behavior or activity from your life. You might try cutting out refined sugar, watching televi-

sion, or something that came to mind while answering the Personal Reflection questions. What do you notice about yourself and your life without the behavior or activity? Are you restless, anxious, more energetic, bored?

PART III

THE HEART
SET FREE

CHAPTER 7

Bravehearts

Welcome to my gallery of bravehearts. At the end of each of the stories in this chapter are a few questions that may help you examine your heart and your choices to allocate and reserve passion. Although the specifics of the stories might differ from your own, I encourage you to "try on" the stories, answer the questions each raises, peer courageously into the dilemmas of each woman, and look for evidence of our God who loves and redeems.

NANCY'S STORY

They looked perfect. The advertising people from Wal-Mart even chose them to represent "The All-American Family." Nancy showed me the photo of her family that Wal-Mart had selected to use in their solid oak picture frames. I couldn't take my eyes off the beautiful family. Every detail in the picture sparkled with the message that dreams come true and people do live happily ever after.

Nancy's husband looked every bit the "man of her dreams" that she had described to me. She'd married her high-school sweetheart, helped him through college and medical school, and worked alongside him as he established a successful practice as a surgeon. Her two children (a son and a daughter) were the spitting images of their father and mother, and they were irresistible in their matching denim shirts and blue jeans. In the photograph, Nancy held their black and white cat while their golden retriever lay in front of the family. Who could ask for anything more?

Nancy recapped the headlines of her life: a handsome, successful husband; two beautiful, healthy children; a prosperous lifestyle; and friends in their church and community. "I had everything I'd always wanted," Nancy concluded. "But something went wrong."

She went on to explain that during their pursuit of the American dream, their marriage had drifted into a state of neglect. Five months after Wal-Mart selected their family picture, Nancy's world began to fall apart. Although Nancy was deeply hurt, she was not really shocked when her husband confessed that he had become involved with another woman.

Nancy surprised me when she continued: "The perfect picture was part of the problem. My obsession with image and control consumed my time and energy and pushed my husband away."

Nancy humbly and honestly began to describe her life ruled by perfectionism: "Rather than relax with my family, I reorganized our back issues of *National Geographic* in chronological order. Instead of talking about our problems, I invited the neighbors over for a dinner party that would impress Martha Stewart. I spent enormous amounts of time worrying about what others thought of me, always playing for approval. I was often unavailable for my husband because I was scurrying about trying to keep the picture perfect. I made the mistake of thinking that if I did everything right, I could keep things from going wrong.

"But my perfectionism didn't stop with expectations for myself. I sat in judgment on everyone in our family, especially my husband. I believed that who we were and what we did were never quite good enough. Our home became a place of constant striving to earn approval."

Nancy recalled a dinner with friends when her husband retold a particularly funny story about their son. Before everyone finished laughing, Nancy interjected: "You got the time and place wrong, but I guess everyone got the gist of the story." Nancy grimaced as she recalled, "It was as if I'd taken a pin and poked a hole in a balloon. My correction deflated the rest of the evening."

I'll never forget Nancy's poignant conclusion: "Perfectionism can break your heart and all the hearts around you."

When she learned of her husband's affair, "the children and I packed up to move to another state, and I thought my life was over." Nancy continued with her story as tears welled in her eyes, "The life I wanted was broken and could never be fixed. I really thought I wanted to die, that I couldn't go on. Boy! Did I have a lot to learn about the resilience and strength of my heart!"

Nancy shook her head as she recalled her first desperate act when she and her children pulled into their new hometown. Before she even unpacked, she walked down to the beach and lay near the water's edge. Fully clothed, she lay in the sand for hours. Even after the tide shifted and the water began to surge over her, Nancy didn't move.

"I prayed a one-sentence prayer," Nancy remembered. "I said, 'God, I'm not moving until you tell me what to do.' I felt like a beached whale," Nancy smiled. "But I was so desperate to hear from God, I didn't care how I looked. That, in and of itself, was the beginning of change for me!

"The words that rolled over me," Nancy continued, "almost in sync with the waves, were: 'Love the Lord your God with all your heart and with all your mind and love your neighbor as yourself. This is the greatest commandment.'

"At first I wondered what it meant for me to obey the greatest commandment during my greatest crisis," Nancy said. "But after more prayer and thought, I stood up, brushed off the sand, and headed for home. I knew I needed to start by taking care of myself and then to seek others for help and companionship, not approval and admiration. I no longer had the energy or the desire to work to create a perfect picture."

Nancy's resolve reminded me of something I'd read recently in Rachel Naomi Remen's *Kitchen Table Wisdom:*

> To seek approval is to have no resting place, no sanctuary.... Approval encourages a constant striving. This is as true of the approval we give ourselves as it is of the approval we offer others. Approval can't be trusted. It can be withdrawn at any time no matter what our track record has been. It is as nourishing of real growth as cotton candy. Yet many of us spend our lives pursuing it.[1]

Nancy knew she needed real sustenance, and so she came up with a plan that included physical exercise, daily quiet time, a weekly massage, and weekly counseling for herself and her children. She and her children found a church, and she selected a small group that she thought would provide support and encouragement. "I was no longer trying to keep everything 'picture perfect' in order to feel whole, but I was learning that living in accordance with God's direction and depending on the support and strength of others resulted in wholeness."

I saw a glimpse of Nancy's brave heart when she admitted, "There were many days when all I wanted to do was pull the blankets over my head and have a marathon pity party, but I determined to obey God's command to take care of myself. And after I exercised or went to my small group, I had more energy to nurture and care for my children." Nancy was experiencing the mystery the apostle Paul describes in Philippians 2:12-13: "Be energetic in your life of salvation, reverent and sensitive before God. That energy is *God's* energy, an energy deep within you, God himself willing and working at what will give him the most pleasure" *(The Message)*.

For two years Nancy lived what she believed was a life of obedience to God's call to her on the beach. She cared for her own heart with the tenderness and attentiveness its wounds needed. She was able to sense her children's needs more readily because of her vigilance with her own heart. In response to her own pain, she cultivated a powerful intuition, an increased sensitivity, and a passionate devotion to others who were hurting. Nancy began to work in a program for the handicapped that taught adults and children with physical as well as emotional disabilities to ride horses. How she loved to watch the growing relationship between instructor, rider, and horse unlock doors to greater confidence and sheer joy.

"Months into my obedience to God's answer, I began to think a lot about my husband and what would become of him," Nancy told me, "and I wanted to pray for him but I didn't know how. The sorrow that welled up in me for all that was lost was almost overwhelming." Nancy explained that all she could do was pray for her husband without words, but with a heart full of longing.

One of the things I love about the Bible's story of Ruth is that although she was "energetic in her life of salvation," when it became necessary for Boaz to act in redeeming Ruth and Naomi, Ruth wasn't involved in the activity. Naomi wisely advised her: "Wait, my daughter, until you find out what happens. For the man will not rest until the matter is settled today" (Ruth 3:18). Nancy's brave heart was in its place of greatest courage as she relinquished control, left her husband in God's hands, and continued on her path of obedience regardless of her husband's actions or others' opinions. Sometimes the most awesome courage is the kind that enables you to live well from one moment to the next, depending on God to work in the people you love. I love what Pastor Jack Hayford writes in *A New Time and Place* about the story of Ruth: "Like Ruth, we are privileged to answer the Spirit's call to depend totally—*totally*—upon our Redeemer. There are times in life when the very best thing we can do is to 'sit still' and let the Redeemer redeem."[2]

Years after Nancy's prayer on the beach, her husband came home. Of course, his return was what Nancy longed for, but because she had spent months wholly engaged in a life committed to "the greatest commandment," she knew that reconciliation would be hard work. She did not want them to slide into a relationship carelessly that would be dishonoring to themselves or each other, even if it looked good from the outside. She asked her husband to begin seeing their pastor for counsel as well as joining her in couple's counseling. They participated in a twenty-week "marriage recovery" course before they began to talk with their pastor about remarriage. Nancy's husband came home to an energetic woman with a heart full of faith, hope, and love, and he quickly discovered that he had to work to win her.

Nancy laughs when she talks about the Wal-Mart picture. "You can hardly find one anymore, unless it's on the clearance rack," she grins. "Not too long ago a friend called to tell me the most amazing story. My friend was attending an evangelistic service, and the traveling evangelist held up *our* Wal-Mart picture! He exhorted, 'Even a perfect family like this can fall apart if they don't pay attention!' And then he threw our picture to the ground, and it broke into hundreds of pieces.

"God has such a sense of humor," Nancy smiles. "I guess the evangelist thought the family in the picture wasn't real. He didn't know it had already fallen apart!"

Nancy's story reminds me why I love women's stories. A fiction writer couldn't make up a story as meaningful and surprising as Nancy's. Nancy would tell you today that she still winces when she remembers parts of her story, and she worries when their marriage grows dull or distant. But she knows that is the time to claim what is deep and true within her, not to get busy organizing her kitchen cupboards! She expresses her longings to her husband and discloses her fears. She is not ashamed of her wounds and reminds herself of the life they awakened within her heart. She renews her prayer life, the disciplines of study and meditation, and she and her husband often seek prayer and counsel from others.

Nancy told me about one of her weekly exercises to combat her perfectionism that I decided I would be wise to include in my regimen. Every week she comes up with a new way to tell the people in her life that they are right, and she uses the phrase as often as possible! Her "phrase of the week" when we last talked was "I wish I had said that."

And she would tell you she has a great life. Not a picture-perfect life. But a life that is fulfilling the deepest dreams of her heart—a life of extravagant love.

Finding Yourself in the Story

1. How important is image to you? What is your ideal image for those things that are important to you, such as your appearance, your marriage, your home, etc.?
2. How much of what you do is controlled by what others think?
3. When you know you are right, do you
   a. let everyone know what you know?
   b. keep quiet and fume?
   c. correct others?
4. When you experience difficulties, demands, or dullness in your relationships, what do you do? Pray fervently and ask God for guidance? Try harder to make things work?

5. Are you consistently setting aside time to listen to God's heart and your own regarding the life of your relationships? If not, why not?

6. In what ways do you work to take care of yourself so you can be free for the work of love?

    __ massage   __ medical evaluation   __ diet

    __ Bible study   __ art class   __ bubble bath

    __ counseling   __ daily quiet time   __ coffee with a friend

    __ support group   __ exercise   __ journaling

7. From whom do you seek help?

    __ pastor   __ friends   __ nutritional counselor

    __ family   __ a dating service   __ fitness/trainer

    __ neighbors   __ career counselor   __ small group

    __ a counselor   __ financial advisor   __ doctor

TERRI'S STORY

Terri came to see me for counseling because she had a sense that life was passing her by. "I look at the people in my church, at my job, even in my neighborhood, and everyone has more of a life than I do."

When I asked Terri to explain what she meant, she listed her grievances: "My best friend got married last year, and she doesn't have as much time for our relationship as she used to, and we don't seem to have as much in common. My coworkers are always talking about their latest vacation or weekend get-together, and all I can contribute to the conversation are highlights of the recent episode of *Law and Order*. My job is meaningless anyway. I meet people who have jobs that make a difference, and mine just barely makes ends meet. My sister just had a baby, and she has no idea how her bundle of joy reminds me of my emptiness." Terri continued to articulate the deficiencies of her life with a hint of humor and an overwhelming sense of sadness.

Terri recalled feeling alienated from others as early as age seven and believing she could never fit in with her classmates. Terri's father left when she was four, and her mother worked two jobs to support their family. Terri spent many afternoons in front of the television—alone. Terri disclosed to me the intense shame she felt about herself and her family and her early determination to "get ahead in the game." In college, Terri studied day and night to get good grades and a chance to move away from her life of poverty and loneliness. "I constantly compared myself to others and worked to surpass their accomplishments. But I didn't have much of a social life. I'm shy and don't talk easily to people. I guess that's a big part of my problem. If you can help me to develop a different personality, maybe then I can have the life I really want."

My heart went out to this likeable woman. She believed that her financial status, her job, being single, and being shy were keeping her from the life she wanted. She didn't know that what was really trapping her was an unhealthy cycle of desire, disappointment, comparison, and contempt.

Terri ended the description of her life situation with an angry exclamation: "I am just so mad about the life I've been stuck with! I hated growing up poor. I hate my father for leaving and my mother for being so busy. I hate how I look, and I hate being shy. It's not fair that everyone else seems to have what I want!" By the time Terri finished speaking she looked exhausted. A heart made hard by comparisons and envy is a heavy weight to lug around.

I handed Terri a small tape recorder and asked her to record her thoughts over the course of the next week whenever she noticed deficiencies in her own life or blessings in the lives of others. When she came for her next appointment, we listened to the tape together. Terri's heart immediately softened when she heard her repeated expressions of envy, anger, pettiness, and self-hatred. She smiled wryly, "I guess shyness is not my biggest personality flaw."

I explained that I didn't think shyness was a flaw at all and that part of her work was to see her innate idiosyncrasies with the same grace and humility as she saw her best qualities. I suggested that weaknesses, unlucky breaks, and even unfair realities can work to our advantage by making us more dependent on God, more resilient, more creative, and ultimately more powerfully engaged in relationships. I asked her to consider the strange joy of the apostle Paul: "I quit focusing on the handicap and began appreciating the gift. It was a case of Christ's strength moving in on my weakness. Now I take limitations in stride, and with good cheer, these limitations that cut me down to size—abuse, accidents, opposition, bad breaks. I just let Christ take over! And so the weaker I get, the stronger I become" (2 Corinthians 12:9-10, *The Message*).

Terri and I talked about her anger with God for creating her with longings that seemed thwarted at every turn. We discussed her pain and fury about the family God placed her in and the personality he gave her. She saw clearly that her response to desire and the often accompanying disappointment was the toxic trio of comparison, envy, and contempt for herself and others. Although Terri ached with loneliness, a chip on her shoulder isolated her further from God and others.

Terri wrestled with these realities for quite some time until she became willing to confess that her comparisons and complaints had only resulted in more disappointments and difficulties and kept her from the life she really wanted. We talked a lot about the peculiar notion that the best response to those hard things over which we have no control is to live well; that is, to respond to them in godly ways.

So often when we are confronted with situations over which we feel powerless—financial strain, being misunderstood, loneliness—we simply don't live well; instead we respond by becoming angry, lashing back, or scheming to regain a sense of control. But true power is found in passionately and persistently living well.

During one of our sessions, Terri talked about the notion of living well with a frustration and fatigue that is familiar to most women: "I'm just so tired. I'm tired of doing all the work. I want someone else to take care of me. I want to lose weight and exercise, but my job is so demanding and stressful all I can do when I get home is collapse in front of the television. I hate my job, but I need the money. I would like to meet people, maybe even a man, but I'm too tired!"

When life seems to fall in on us and we are in despair, we should honor our heart's cry for help and acknowledge that the choices we are making on a daily level are about life and death. I asked Terri if she could admit that she was in a life-and-death situation and begin making choices to live.

Terri's first choice was to get a medical evaluation. Her doctor recommended that she begin taking an antidepressant. At first Terri resisted, fearing that an antidepressant was a sign that she was weak. Her doctor told her that pain, whether it is physical or emotional, is instructive, and tells us that something has to change before all of our energy is spent simply enduring, numbing, or avoiding the pain.

After about six weeks of taking care of herself physically, Terri made a significant decision. She decided to quit her high-stress job. She gave her notice at work and made plans to move into a smaller, less expensive apartment. She decided to spend a year working for a temporary agency so that she could sift through job possibilities and do something she really wanted to do. During her year of temporary assignments, Terri started to dream.

Terri disclosed two dreams that she'd always held very dear, but imagined would never be realized: (1) she wanted to work in a helping or caregiving profession, and (2) she wanted to get married. For six months Terri prayed about her dreams before she told anyone what she longed for. Then she decided to give feet to her hopes.

Terri applied for a job as a receptionist and volunteer coordinator for a large hospice center. When I asked her if she was sure this job matched her own gifts and "people skills," she replied with an answer that continues to encourage me in my own moments of awkward shyness. "Our physical design ensures that we keep our attention on what's in front of us. Our eyes face forward, like headlights. I think God designed us this way to help us stay involved with someone besides ourselves." Terri continued to instruct and delight me: "I've been practicing looking ahead when I enter the room, making eye contact, being the first to say hello, and smiling at people." Terri's energy was no longer consumed by comparisons and contempt, and so she was free to work at transforming her own limitations into something positive and life-giving.

Her second dream, of being married, was scarier for Terri to talk about. She was over forty years old. She was afraid people would think she was a fool. She began by telling a few close friends that she wanted to date. She asked them to pray and to be sure to introduce her to any single men they knew. Her request required more vulnerability and courage than any appeal for help she'd ever made. Terri laughed when she said to me, "The best thing that ever happened to me was to discover that I have abilities, gifts, and dreams. And the worst thing that ever happened to me was to discover that I have abilities, gifts, and dreams!" Acknowledging our longings and viewing them as holy compels us to take action. Passivity, although lonely and powerless, is far less risky.

Terri decided to place an ad with a Christian singles network. When asked to describe herself, she wrote:

I polled some friends when I decided to do this and they said I am: real, passionate, bright, vulnerable, shy, creative, I know where I've been, I'm willing to share my heart, I'm humorous (really!), and I speak honestly. I promise that all of this feedback came from real people and no one received any monetary compensation for their comments!

I couldn't help but note the dramatic change in Terri's attitude toward herself. The best beauty product is a life surrendered to the challenges, disappointments, and blessings of our unique situation with a belief in God's goodness, a willingness to accept our responsibility, and a sense of humor.

As men began to respond to her ad, she had some pretty horrible first dates. Her sense of humor and determination to keep trying reveal her amazing, brave heart. She's also had some fun dates, and she's made an important discovery. Terri explained to me that she had postponed living most of her life. She believed that "when I get married, then I'll be happy." As she got older and let that dream die, she continued to postpone, living with "when I lose weight, then I'll be happy. When I get a different job, then I'll be happy. When I get my house decorated just right, then I'll be happy."

"I've decided," Terri concluded, "to live while I'm alive! I'm not going to stop dreaming and pursuing my dreams, but I'm going to enjoy what I'm in the midst of right now too!"

I know Terri would tell you that she has a great life—a life that is no longer passing her by, but one in which she is living and loving her dreams into reality.

Finding Yourself in the Story

1. What kind of life do you want? What is keeping you from having that kind of life?

2. How often do you evaluate your life by comparing it to someone else's?

3. When you are overwhelmed by circumstances that are out of your control, what is your response?

4. What does it mean for you to live well?

5. Write your own ad introducing yourself. What does it say about how you view your life?

Julie's Story

"I might as well have been on drugs," Julie surprised me with this answer when I asked about her job. I bumped into Julie in the foyer after church one Sunday and realized it had been over two years since we'd last talked. Julie worked as the advertising and marketing director for a local Christian college. She was perfect for the job. Julie is a high-energy woman who has a sense of what people like and what motivates them to action. When she was promoted from assistant director to the head of advertising, we'd celebrated with a cup of coffee at our favorite coffee shop. I'd identified with her satisfaction: "It feels so good to have my ideas and efforts rewarded!" We laughed together about the reality that family often overlooks our accomplishments and they never pay us for our time!

"What do you mean?" I asked Julie in response to her strange answer about her job.

"Success and satisfaction at work became an obsession. They started to run my life and control how I felt every second of the day. Even when I wasn't at work, I was thinking about my job and how I could make things better. I told myself after the 'next project,' things would get back to normal, but that way of life becomes habit-forming—and exhausting. My job started to control my mood, feelings about my self-worth, energy level, motivation level, *my life!*"

I could easily identify with some of the things Julie felt. I thought of the many times I'd offered my children advice, and they'd given me "the look" and responded, "Oh, Mom, you just don't understand." I'd felt tempted to remind them: "I'm a counselor. I give people advice for a living. And not only do they want my advice, they pay me!" When clients appreciate and respect me, I'm tempted to spend more time in my office and less time in my living room.

"What happened?" I asked Julie, wanting to know as much for her as for myself.

"I got a wake-up call when I came home from work one Saturday afternoon to find a police car parked in my driveway."

Julie told me she raced from her car into her home fearing what the police car meant. She entered her living room to find a somber group of people. Her two sons sat on the couch with their babysitter while the police officer wrote on his clipboard. Julie breathed a sigh of relief that everyone was present and accounted for and asked, "What's going on?"

"I'm so sorry," the babysitter began. "I was in the house playing with Josh, and I thought Ryan was out front riding bikes with the neighbors. I should have checked on him. I'm so sorry." The babysitter started to cry, and Julie looked at Ryan, her eleven-year-old, who was staring out the window and fighting back tears.

"Your son got ahold of a can of spray paint," the police officer spoke sternly. "He painted an entire wall on one of the buildings in the park. We have to take this seriously. It's vandalism."

He handed Julie a paper and her mind was racing, like a videotape on rewind, as she replayed the events of the summer. Ryan had been in trouble a lot. He threw rocks at their house, breaking a window. He stole some baseball cards from a neighbor that she'd made him return when she discovered them in Ryan's bedroom. He picked fights with his brother incessantly. Julie silently chastised herself, "Why didn't I see what was happening!"

She looked at the paper in front of her. It was a summons. Ryan was being charged with a crime and had to appear before a judge in a week! Julie mumbled something—she doesn't remember what she said—to the police officer and he left. Then she turned to look at her son. His tears turned to defiance and he shouted, "Go ahead and put me in a foster home! Then you won't have to worry about me anymore." Ryan ran to his room and slammed the door.

Julie was speechless. She told me her first thoughts were, "This is all my fault. I've been a terrible mother, only thinking of my job and myself."

Julie was face to face with a moment of truth. When Julie arrived home to a challenging situation, she had a choice. She could chalk up Ryan's behavior as another discouragement in parenting and echo what I hear struggling women express often: "Why even try? This is overwhelming!" But while taking the role of victim may at times feel justified, it is never empowering.

Julie courageously chose a different response to the surprise in her living room. She asked her other son to go to his room, and she got on her knees in front of the couch. She knew her obsession with work had kept her from being actively involved with her sons. Julie asked God for forgiveness for the past and strength for the present. Whatever the difficulties we face in our relationships, we must begin by telling ourselves the truth about our responsibility for the condition of those relationships. Julie honestly laid out her sin before God. She confessed her selfishness, her disappointment and even anger with her family, and her determination to find a life that satisfied and affirmed her, even at the expense of those she loved. She smiled when she said it, but with tears streaming down her face, she asked God her son's desperate question: "God, do you want to put me in foster care?"

Julie told me that after praying she still did not know how to deal with her son. She picked up her Bible and turned to the Psalms. After turning a few pages, she began to read Psalm 139, and found words that settled her heart and gave her direction for her son:

> O LORD, you have searched me
> > and you know me.
> You know when I sit and when I rise;
> > you perceive my thoughts from afar.
> You discern my going out and my lying down;
> > you are familiar with all my ways.
> Before a word is on my tongue
> > you know it completely, O LORD.
> You hem me in—behind and before;
> > you have laid your hand upon me.
> Such knowledge is too wonderful for me,
> > too lofty for me to attain.
> Where can I go from your Spirit?
> > Where can I flee from your presence?
> If I go up to the heavens, you are there;
> > If I make my bed in the depths, you are there.
> If I rise on the wings of the dawn,
> > if I settle on the far side of the sea,

even there your hand will guide me,
    your right hand will hold me fast.
If I say, "Surely the darkness will hide me
    and the light become night around me,"
even the darkness will not be dark to you;
    the night will shine like the day,
    for darkness is as light to you.

Julie knocked on Ryan's door with fear and trembling, but with a clear picture of extravagant love. She hugged him tightly and looked him right in the eyes: "Foster care is the last thing on my mind. We are going to spend more time together than you ever thought possible. Where you go, I go. We will find our way out of this together." Julie apologized to her son for not paying attention and assured him that she loved him and wanted to help him.

The following week Julie and Ryan went to court, and Ryan was sternly lectured by the judge and sentenced to ten hours of community service. The judge suggested they call churches or other nonprofit organizations to see if Ryan could do his community service for them. Julie began to call as soon as they got home. She called over a dozen organizations and discovered that finding a place for Ryan to serve was not going to be easy. Most organizations were concerned with their responsibility and potential liability for an eleven-year-old boy. They explained to Julie that their insurance would not allow them to employ Ryan, even on a volunteer basis. Julie called her own church, which offered the opportunity for Ryan to pull weeds, but that would take less than an hour. Julie started to get discouraged. The court ordered that Ryan complete his community service within one week.

Once again Julie fought the impulse to respond to her circumstances with a sense of "Nothing ever works out. Life is not fair!" She determined to stay in the tension of Philippians 2:12, that when we work, we experience God and he energizes us to love others. She called Ryan and Josh in from playing outside and suggested, "Let's take a walk, and while we walk we'll pray and ask God for help."

While walking in their neighborhood, Julie stopped in front of a neighbor's house she'd seen a thousand times, but today she saw it with new eyes. The yard was overgrown with grass and weeds. The driveway and garage were so cluttered that the car was parked on the street and the garage doors couldn't shut. "I have an idea," Julie spoke with quiet confidence. "Let's go call the judge."

Julie explained her idea to the clerk at the courthouse. Julie knew the house with the yard in disrepair belonged to another single mom with small children. She asked the clerk if Ryan could do this neighbor's yard work for his community service. The court reluctantly agreed.

You can imagine the neighbor's surprise when Julie, Josh, and Ryan showed up on her doorstep with lawn tools, trash bags, and an eagerness to do chores that had gone undone for months. The neighbor signed the papers for the court with heartfelt gratitude that she had benefited from Julie's hardship. They promised to meet for coffee soon. That night over pizza, Julie and her boys talked about how much fun it was to work together and do something for someone in need.

Julie told me that out of their crisis, she and her sons began S.O.S.— Help for Hurting Families. They started out by doing chores around the house for families in need about once a month. They have such fun choosing the family to help, planning their work, and working together. Julie, who has never been much of a handywoman, is learning a lot about tools and repair jobs and is on a first-name basis with the manager at the local hardware store. When he learned about their projects, he asked if he could get others involved.

Over the past year, Julie and her troops have helped build decks (a local squad of firefighters has made building decks for low-income families an annual project in partnership with Julie and her sons); shopped for and delivered boxes of groceries; painted houses, inside and out; mowed lawns and pulled weeds; and spent afternoons playing games with small children to give single moms a break.

Julie invited me to a cookout for all her volunteers, and the next Saturday I joined over 125 people crowded into Julie's backyard! I watched with utter respect and delight as Julie and her sons served their volunteers. I caught a few special looks between Julie and Ryan—a mother and son so proud of each other. Julie continues to work in advertising at the college, but now she is reserving energy and using her gifts in the context of relationships instead of being consumed by the vicious cycle of self-gratification. I know Julie and her sons would say they have a great life— a life filled with family and friends and meaningful work together.

Finding Yourself in the Story

1. In what ways might you be bending your life away from God and toward affairs of the heart?
2. In what area do you feel a need that seems out of your control?
3. When have you resolved to give up, cut back, or change the nature of a behavior or relationship and been unable to follow through?
4. As you examine your relationships, can you admit your responsibility for what has gone wrong? Why or why not?

Transformed Hearts

The stories in this chapter reveal three characteristics of a braveheart. Brave-hearts are willing to wait, to ask, and to act. Extravagant love waits—weeks, months, even years. It is a continuing story that is not chased away by pain and is confident of living and loving *within* the pain. Waiting strengthens faith. Extravagant love asks for help, another chance, support, and opportunity. Asking energizes hope. Extravagant love acts, changing even if those we love do not. Extravagant love embraces the truth that as we love, we discover love. Acting demonstrates love. Waiting, asking, acting—faith, hope, love. And the greatest of these is love.

LIVING IN LOVE

For Personal Reflection and Discussion

1. What behaviors and/or relationships steal your attention and replace your concern for loving God? loving others? loving yourself?

2. Describe how you got to where you are today in your relationships with others and with God.

3. When you are overwhelmed by relationships and responsibilities do you become

   angry   passive   prayerful   sarcastic   active

4. How do you finish the following sentence? "I will be fulfilled, happy, and satisfied when _____."

Into Action

1. In what creative ways can you commit to live out Psalm 139 or Ruth 1:16-17 in your relationships?

2. Spend a week keeping track of your time. Include time spent day-dreaming, tossing and turning at night, worrying, and praying. What subjects, activities, relationships, or beliefs get the greatest percentage of your time?

3. How can you give feet to your dreams? Sometimes it helps to write your dream at the top of a page and then make a list of all the mini-steps necessary to get to your goal. Try that this week.

CHAPTER 8

A Redeemed Heart

Before our hearts can be set free to fully embrace extravagant love, we must ask God to help us clearly recognize our captive hearts. We cannot be free until we know what has carried us away. Only then can we offer our captive hearts to God for his redemptive, transforming love.

One of my favorite stories in the Gospels is the story about a woman caught in sin. We don't know all the details of her story or her sin. I have imagined a few details between the lines we are given in Scripture. We do know that in the end she stands before a crowded room utterly exposed and at the mercy of strangers.

Two men led her into a room filled with people she didn't know. When they first entered the room, she thought they might sit quietly at the back since the meeting had already begun. But the two men marched her to the front, and all eyes shifted from the speaker to them. Her face flushed during this conspicuous entrance, and she fought to hold back tears of fear and humiliation. She could not believe this was happening.

The night before she'd slipped out of her own house to meet a man for a midnight tryst. She knew it was wrong and even dangerous, but the thrill of his touch and the comfort of his kindness enticed her to dismiss her nagging conscience and ignore the possible consequences. Her heart beat faster as she remembered their passionate embrace…and then the loud knock on the door. It had all happened so quickly. Men she recognized as important leaders in their community rushed into the room and commanded her to gather her belongings and to come with them immediately. They'd escorted her through the city, arriving at the meeting at dawn.

She glanced at the man seated at the front of the room and wondered if he was to be her judge. She looked into his eyes imploringly as her escorts told her to stand and face the group. Slowly she turned and saw the crowd sitting on the edge of their seats staring at her. One of her accusers addressed the man sitting before them: "Teacher, this woman was caught in the act of adultery. In the Law Moses commanded us to stone such women. Now what do you say?" (adapted from John 8)

I wonder if you've ever read this story in John's gospel and put yourself in the role of this woman. Caught. Exposed. All eyes on you.

There's something about having your darkest secrets revealed like this that stirs memories of my mother catching me in a lie, a teacher finding me unprepared, or a friend hurt by my careless words. I've even had dreams about arriving at school, church, or work in only a slip, trying desperately to find my dress before someone catches me improperly clothed.

Do you understand the picture? If you do, then Jesus' response is the most relieving and extravagant gesture imaginable. The passage tells us that

Jesus bent down to write something in the dirt. The crowd continued to hammer him with questions and accusations about her crime and punishment. He straightened up, looked at them and said, "If any one of you is without sin, let him be the first to throw a stone at her" (8:7).

And then as if to underscore his heart for this woman, "Again he stooped down and wrote on the ground" (8:8).

I have heard pastors and theologians debate and speculate about what Jesus wrote in the dirt, but I cannot get past his gesture of stooping before the woman while everyone else sat ramrod straight in their chairs expecting an execution.

At last, after everyone had filed out, Jesus straightened himself and asked: "Woman, where are they? Has no one condemned you?"

"No one, sir," she said.

"Then neither do I condemn you," Jesus declared. "Go now and leave your life of sin" (8:9-11).

Jesus describes his revolutionary encounter with the captive heart: "I tell you most solemnly that anyone who chooses a life of sin is trapped in a dead-end life and is, in fact, a slave. A slave is a transient, who can't come and go at will. The Son, though, has an established position, the run of the house. So if the Son sets you free, you are free through and through" (8:34-36, *The Message*).

Can you imagine all that stirred in the adulterous woman's heart as she looked into the eyes of her Savior and saw only compassion and forgiveness? The redeemed heart is set free to exclaim with the psalmist: "Before the 'gods' I will sing your praise. I will bow down toward your holy temple and will praise your name for your love and your faithfulness.... When I called, you answered me; you made me bold and stouthearted" (Psalm 138:1-3).

Moments of Truth

The heart is set free to love extravagantly only after being caught and exposed. This is different from the captivity we looked at in part 2. There we examined choices and behaviors that imprison our hearts and keep us from loving freely and fully. Now we're talking about how being caught reveals our captivity to negative thoughts or behaviors. As we've looked at affairs and entanglements of the heart, perfectionism and controlling behavior, heart-hardening comparison, envy, and gossip, have you felt caught as you've identified some of your own sinful choices? Or perhaps in the discussion about our longings to love and be loved, you've felt exposed by the discovery of your own desires. Maybe you've thought to yourself, "I didn't know anyone else felt that way" or "Oh, that's exactly what I want."

Being caught involves more than our sin finding us out. It also includes our being known, exposed, and confronted by the truth about ourselves, both good and bad. And once we are caught, whether it be as dramatically as the woman in John 8 or more subtly in the privacy of our own quiet reflection, we are at a crossroads—a moment of truth.

Moments of truth come in all sizes and shapes and at all hours of the day or night. Not long ago a friend lamented to me, "A good marriage takes too much work! I try to be creative and my husband doesn't even notice. I quit! I just can't do this anymore. If all he wants are evenings with Dan Rather and Monday Night Football, then that's what he'll get!"

We commiserated for a few minutes about lonely Monday nights and the conspiracy by the National Football League to destroy, or at least undermine, marriage, and then we changed the subject. A few weeks later my husband and I received an invitation in the mail to a Monday Night Football party at this friend's house. She'd invited six couples to come over for dinner and the game with two stipulations: (1) The wives must actively watch every minute of the game, and (2) the husbands must spend every minute of commercials talking about subjects of the wives' choice. I called my friend to RSVP and teased, "So much for giving up on marriage! You are so committed to your husband and relationships that you'll even use football!"

This bravehearted woman was caught—caught in her resilience, creativity, and commitment to relationships and caught in her foolishness for believing she could harden her heart toward her husband and the life of their marriage.

Moments of truth, no matter how dramatic or ordinary, can result in denial or understanding and lead to resentment or repentance. Which path we choose in these defining moments determines whether our heart is free to love extravagantly.

The apostle Paul expresses it passionately: "Dear, dear Corinthians, I can't tell you how much I long for you to enter this wide-open, spacious life.... The smallness you feel comes from within you. Your lives aren't small, but you're living them in a small way. I'm speaking as plainly as I can and with great affection. Open up your lives. Live openly and expansively!" (2 Corinthians 6:11-13, *The Message*).

THE POWER OF YOUR STORY

Most of the women who come to me for counseling express a common desire for the outcome of their therapy: "I want to know who I am." Counselors often get a bad rap for spending too much time in the past, but I believe that knowing, accepting, and understanding one's story is the beginning of extravagant love.

Verses 2 and 3 of Proverbs 2 urge us to turn our ears to wisdom and apply our hearts to understanding, to call out for insight and cry aloud for understanding. In his book *Reaching Out*, Henri Nouwen writes about the benefits of knowing yourself:

> What if the events of our history are molding us as a sculptor molds his clay, and if it is only in a careful obedience to these molding hands that we can discover our real vocation and become mature people? What if all the unexpected interruptions are in fact invitations to give up old-fashioned and out-moded styles of living and are opening up new unexplored areas of experience? And finally: What if our history does not prove to be a blind impersonal sequence of events over which we have no control, but rather reveals to us a guiding hand pointing to a personal encounter in which all our hopes and aspirations will reach their fulfillment? Then our life would indeed be different, because then fate becomes opportunity, wounds a warning, and paralysis an invitation to search for deeper sources of vitality.[1]

Understanding your story involves not only delving into the past but inevitably leads to analyzing the present. What have the wounds, joys, disappointments, and discoveries of the past led you to choose in the present? I pray that this book, so far, has encouraged you to search for the moments in your story that have made a difference in the trajectory of your life so that you've come to an understanding about the state of your relationships. Have you been able to admit your holy longing for relationships and confess the foolish and wise, sinful and righteous, apathetic and passionate choices you've made in response to that longing?

Acknowledging our longings and confessing our responses can be humbling and terrifying, but I can testify that the heart is set free only as we tell our story truthfully with insight and understanding. This takes reflection, prayer, courage, and sometimes the help of a counselor, pastor, or friend.

Years ago I found myself in a moment of truth that has determined the course of my story ever since. As I've already shared with you, I was trapped in alcohol dependency, running from the joy and pain of relationships to a numbing substance that kept me from freely loving and fully living. I kept my struggle a secret because I was a Christian and feared that the revelation of my addiction would result in the loss of friends, reputation, and ministry.

I knew my relationships with family, friends, and God were deteriorating, but I vigorously denied, to myself, that confession of my sin and story would do any good in restoring these relationships. I felt awful about myself but refused to look openly and honestly at my persistent self-destruction. When a made-for-TV movie about alcohol abuse came on, I'd turn the channel. When I flipped through women's magazines and saw a headline about alcoholism, I quickly turned the page. My heart was closed to understanding.

One Sunday after a particularly convicting message at church, I prayed, "God, help me." It was a small moment of truth when my heart opened a fraction of an inch. From that moment on I could not shake nagging questions about my story. I had always known my mother was adopted, but neither my mother nor I had ever pursued any information about her birth parents. Two weeks after my prayer in church, I called my mom and pleaded, "I need to know about your birth mother." I could not articulate the reasons. It seemed crazy, but my life curled into this one compelling question.

My mom searched through her papers and provided me with her birth certificate and certificate of adoption. She shrugged her shoulders and said, "Go ahead, see what you can find out."

The birth certificate listed my mom's birth mother's name as Marjorie Clay Dixon. My mom also knew that her mother was a student at the University of Wyoming when she'd become pregnant. I obtained a current listing of the University of Wyoming alumni with addresses and telephone numbers. I randomly selected the number of someone who would have attended the university when Marjorie was a student.

The elderly woman who answered the phone remembered "Marj" and recalled her older brother, Edward Clay. Unbelievably, the directory listed an "Edward Clay" with a California telephone number.

Suddenly I was afraid, and so I handed the telephone to my husband! He called Mr. Clay and gently asked about Marjorie. The poor man was completely baffled by my husband's inquiries and suggested we call Marjorie's daughter Susan, who lived only sixty miles from our home!

I called Susan and falteringly attempted to explain my interest in her mother. Susan was neither shocked nor surprised. Although her mother never talked openly about the baby girl she gave away, Susan had discovered her mother's secret and watched it haunt her mother throughout her life.

My heart beat faster. I knew I was close to understanding more of my own story, and I couldn't stop now. "Where is Marjorie? I'd love to meet her, to talk to her."

Susan's answer stunned me. "My mother died several years ago," she explained with a trace of bitterness. "She was only fifty-two. At the end, she was a hopeless, hallucinating drunk."

Time stopped. I don't remember how the phone call ended. I was caught. The sad story of Marjorie Clay Dixon compelled me to tell myself the truth about my own life. I was an alcoholic, and Marjorie's story of broken relationships, impoverished children, insane paranoia, numerous hospitalizations, and bleak funeral was like a malignant prophecy. When my story collided with Marjorie's, God was answering my cry for help. My heart that had opened a sliver to understanding suddenly opened wide.

I could have just as easily retreated to denial. Denial becomes a haven when we believe our sin is too great—or too small—to withstand scrutiny from God and others. My own hidden life of alcohol dependency had seemed too "big" a problem to confess and expect healing and forgiveness. My friend's desire to harden her heart against her football-fanatic husband seemed too "small" at first for her to bother with. But denial, on a large or small scale, not only closes the heart to acknowledgment of sin but also denies us the fruit of repentance, which is a heart set free for extravagant love.

After discovering my family history of alcoholism, I bowed my head and acknowledged aloud: "Lord, I am a sinner. A broken and needy woman. I am caught in the disease of alcoholism and I see no way out. I need your mercy and your grace."

I took consolation in Jesus' words to the woman in the gospel story: "Neither do I condemn you. Go now and leave your life of sin." Of course, a lot of hard work lay ahead, but in that moment, understanding and repentance opened my heart for redemption.

Learning your story and understanding your life choices is wholly worthwhile because it provides the most meaningful context for repentance.

The Rewards of Repentance

I'll never forget the woman who came to see me for help with a gambling addiction. She learned to escape a difficult marriage by making the short drive from Denver to the mountain casinos. She confessed that she was spending three thousand dollars every other day at the slot machines! She came to see me because her debts had caught up with her. *She* was caught. With shoulders slumped and eyes downcast, she moaned, "I just can't believe what a mess I've made of things…my family, our finances, my marriage. I am nothing but a failure."

I responded kindly, "You're wrong. You are much more than a failure. But you *are* a failure."

I could almost see her heart snap shut as she sat up straight, looked me right in the eyes, and defiantly asked, "What do you mean, I'm a failure?"

We are afraid of admitting our failures, frailties, and foolishness. Who wants to admit that they envy and gossip, obsess about appearance, give up on relationships, or become entangled with destructive attachments? When relationships are disappointing or unsatisfying, it is not natural for us to follow the psalmist in asking God to search our hearts for any offensive actions that might be at the root of our troubles (Psalm 139:23-24).

It doesn't take a great deal of reflection and understanding to realize that we long for so much in relationships that has not been fulfilled or that seems out of our reach. Sadly, when this realization dawns, many of us jump from understanding to resentment rather than to repentance. We wonder why we don't have what we want. We blame others or God for the disappointments. We become cynical and critical. Resentment unites anger, fear, and sadness in a vicious cycle that ultimately refuses relationship and isolates us from others. Resentment echoes Peter's query in Matthew 18:21, "Lord, how many times shall I forgive my brother when he sins against me?" *How many times do I need to be hurt?* Resentment determines to never risk or experience the pain of relationships again.

But Scripture clearly teaches that good fruit grows out of confession and repentance. Matthew 3:11 claims that repentance sets us free to exchange our old lives for kingdom lives *(The Message)*. Repentance produces a heart turned to God (Acts 26:20), a radical life change (Romans 2:4), intimacy with God (2 Corinthians 7:9), and a life without regret (2 Corinthians 7:10). Second Timothy 2:25-26 gives us the wondrous promise that repentance allows us to turn to the truth, enabling us to escape the devil's trap, where we are caught and held captive *(The Message)*. These fruits of repentance are rooted not only in our initial salvation, but continue to be cultivated in our ongoing walk with God as we are sensitive to our need to confess our sins and actively seek forgiveness. A repentant heart is open to God, intimately connected with him, always living in the light of the truth, and free to radically love others without regret or limitation!

The practical rewards of a heart bowed in repentance are evident in Lorraine's story. Lorraine came to see me for counseling because she was lonely and wanted help in developing relationships.

"I just don't know where to meet the right people," she explained. "I don't know anyone that I connect with in a meaningful way."

She began to describe the people in her life. According to Lorraine, her coworkers were unbelievers and couldn't talk about spiritual matters, the fellow-members of her Sunday school class were all depressed and not interested in the same activities she was, and the women in her Bible study were too concerned with superficial matters like decorating and golf.

As Lorraine continued, it became evident that she was an expert at finding flaws in people. I asked her if she believed these imperfect people in her life had anything to offer her. When she said, "Not really," I asked her how she thought her standoffishness made them feel. It didn't take long for her to see clearly how she quickly judged others, wrote them off, and made them feel inferior.

Lorraine's good heart became evident as she admitted that it was primarily her self-righteousness and lack of interest in others that had kept her from meaningful relationships. I'll never forget her eloquent repentance:

"It's not a matter of my finding the right people after all, but of my being the right person with the people I've already found!"

Lorraine's relationships changed almost immediately. She began to go to lunch with her coworkers, and soon they were not only supporting one another at work but also joining one another for engagements after work. Lorraine's coworkers are curious about her faith, and Lorraine is excited about future opportunities to share her beliefs. Lorraine organized a ministry from her Sunday school that has bonded them together in significant ways. The class found a struggling inner-city family to adopt and help with home improvements, tutoring for their children, and providing groceries and other supplies. Lorraine discovered that the members of her class were not only talented but compassionate people. They have had such fun ministering together! And Lorraine is learning to play golf. She still doesn't like it much, but she's discovered wandering around a golf course for several hours provides an opportunity for wonderful conversations. Just last week Lorraine said to me, "I think I'm ready to quit counseling. I really don't have time for it anymore!"

THE LIBERATION OF FORGIVENESS

How exactly does repentance open our hearts to extravagant love? Jesus answers this question plainly in Luke 7:47, where he essentially says, "The woman who has been forgiven extravagantly loves extravagantly." Repentance unlocks our hearts so that we can experience the forgiveness that sets us free to love with abandon.

In his essay "A Reflection on Guilt," Dominic Maruca explains:

The memory of things past is indeed a worm that does not die. Whether it continues to grow by gnawing away at our hearts or is

metamorphosed into a brightly colored winged creature depends...
on whether we can find a forgiveness we cannot bestow on
ourselves.[2]

The paltry, pinched heart is transformed into a lavish, loving heart by
forgiveness. The mystery of repentance is that in the process of being loved
by a God who extravagantly forgives, we become extravagant lovers.

Do you find yourself friendless, loveless, cynical, isolated, despairing of
ever enjoying fulfilling relationships? Do you recount your hurts and rehearse the sins against you? Do you look at others and imagine they have
better marriages, children, and friendships than you do? Have you fled
from healthy relationships to destructive ones, believing that's the best you
can do? Resentment is the poison of the life of love. And being forgiven
through repentance is the only antidote for a sick and dying love life.

I discovered the most amazing study about relationships from a group
of Seattle University scholars. The study recruited blatantly victimized
people as well as individuals with more ordinary stories to examine how
people choose to risk, forgive, and engage in meaningful relationships. The
study followed most closely those individuals who initially expressed skep-
ticism about ever forgiving those who had harmed them or even risking in
relationships again.

After varying intervals of time, the researchers discovered one com-
monality among those who were able to let go of the past and become
involved in relationships again. They noted, without exception, that the
resentment had disappeared only when individuals recognized that they
themselves had been forgiven for some offense. Only in receiving forgiveness could they begin to consider forgiving others.

The study told the story of one woman who had experienced childhood abuse and was reluctant to trust anyone fully, resulting in difficulties

in her marriage and other relationships. No matter how hard she tried, she could neither forgive those who had hurt her in the past nor trust those involved with her in the present. She explained that her life changed dramatically when she became involved with a man at the office and her husband found out about it.

I thought, "There it all goes, I've really blown it. I'll probably lose not only him but even the kids."…and you know what? I mean, you probably won't believe this, but he forgave me! We were sitting there one night, after the kids were in bed, and I saw this determination on his face, and I figured, "Here it comes—now I hear about the divorce lawyer." But instead he came over and put his arms around me and started crying and said he didn't want to lose me forever, and could we just close the door on that thing at work and try to be lovers ourselves again?

Well, I could hardly believe it. I just couldn't believe it! But somehow, that's how it's been working out. Oh, we still have our ups and down and our spats about the kids and all, but hey, we're making it! And it's so good to know that he loves me even though I did that, to know that he's forgiven me. I guess that's what has allowed me to forgive those who've hurt me. I really forgive them! I feel so free in all my relationships. I never really thought about it, but I guess it's all connected.[3]

This secular study confirms ancient truth: Extravagant forgiveness frees the heart for extravagant love!

How long has it been since you reveled in the truth of God's extravagant forgiveness? Sadly, for many Christians the rich experience of forgiveness takes place only at salvation. No wonder our hearts grow cold, resentful, and eke out mere pittances of love. The gift of my addiction to alcohol was a radical experience of forgiveness and a heart open to a continual awareness of my foolishness and failures and my need for God's mercy and grace.

As you ponder the state of your relationships, what is your greatest need? What do you want most? Revenge? Affirmation? Understanding? Different people in your life? So often when Christ encountered people in need, before he addressed their "symptoms" he spoke to their greatest need with words that set their hearts free: "Your sins are forgiven" (Matthew 9:2,5; Mark 2:5,9; Luke 7:47-48). The apostle Paul underscores that the deepest need of the human heart is not for a change of circumstances or for human vindication, but for divine forgiveness. "When you were stuck in your old sin-dead life, you were incapable of responding to God. God brought you alive [through his forgiveness].... Think of it! All sins forgiven" (Colossians 2:13, *The Message*). That is why God is relentless in pursuing us—to catch us in our need of him.

A few years ago I heard a story, one of those urban legends, that illustrates wonderfully how being caught in the light of truth can literally save one's life. The story is of a single mother, heading home after a long day at the office. She is tired and anticipating a busy evening of picking up her children from day care, preparing dinner, and getting ready to do it all over again the next day. When she gets into her car to head home, she notices that she is almost out of gas. It feels like the last straw to have to stop and get gas before fulfilling all the rest of her evening's duties, but she pulls over at the first gas station on her way home.

As soon as she leaves the gas station, she notices a car following her closely. She speeds up. The other car speeds up as well. She changes lanes.

The other car not only changes lanes behind her, but also flashes its bright lights in her rearview mirror. She changes lanes again, and the other car follows her, its headlights glaring into the back of her car.

By this time her heart is pounding and her mind is racing with the news report she heard earlier that day. She recalls the warning that a man is forcing women in their cars to the side of the highway through various means and kidnapping and assaulting them. She visualizes the route she will take, not to her children's day care, but to the nearest police station. She anxiously plans how she will pull up to the front door and jump into the safety of the station…if the car continues to follow.

And it does. It follows her off the highway, through the twists and turns of the neighborhood, and into the parking lot of the police station. Its bright headlights taunt her right up to the front door.

She dashes into the safety of the lighted building, screaming, "Help me! Help me! Someone is following me."

In a flash the man in the pursuing car runs into the station and joins her there.

"That's him!" she screams. "That's the man who was following me!"

He kindly grabs her by the arm and motions for her to calm down. "Come with me," he invites.

He leads her and a police officer to her car and explains, "I saw a man get into your car at the gas station when you stopped. When he crouched in the back seat, I knew he intended to harm you. I followed, flashing my headlights to try to get your attention and warn you of the danger."

Like this conscientious friend, God pursues us, sometimes silently and sometimes shouting. The light of his love is sometimes dimmed and sometimes glaring. He sometimes uses the danger of relationships to stop us, catch us, and reveal to us how much we need him. Through confession and repentance, we experience the joy of his liberating grace.

We can consistently experience the profound forgiveness that opens our hearts to extravagant love by being willing to see the truth about our own sin and by consciously depending upon God's forgiveness in everyday life. Keeping our hearts open to redemption happens through discipline. As we will see in the next chapter, it is only through practice that we gain the heart skills to love extravagantly.

LIVING IN LOVE

For Personal Reflection or Discussion

1. Have you experienced a moment of truth while reading this book? In what ways have you been "caught" in the truth about yourself, either good or bad?
2. Do you know your own story? What events have molded you? What wounds, joys, disappointments, or discoveries have made a difference in the course of your life?
3. When have you said to yourself, "I will never put myself in a position to be hurt again"? What prompted that conclusion?
4. Describe an experience of forgiveness that has been life changing.
5. What have you considered your greatest need?

Into Action

1. Put yourself in God's stories. Turn to a passage of Scripture that shows God's extravagant forgiveness, such as Jesus and the woman caught in adultery (John 7:53–8:11, the Old Testament picture of Christ's sacrifice for our sins (Isaiah 53), or a New Testament passage detailing the Crucifixion (John 19). Enter the passage through meditation, placing yourself in the story, as I modeled for

you earlier in the account from John's gospel, and then let Jesus speak to you personally, offering words of mercy, forgiveness, and guidance.

2. Put God in your stories. Meditate on a specific time when God has forgiven you in the past. I often encourage women to write about their most shame-filled moment and describe in detail every smell, sight, sound, and touch of the event. Put God in the story, asking for a sense of the fullness of his unconditional love and forgiveness that "purifies us from all unrighteousness" (1 John 1:9).

3. Take out a piece of paper and write down everything you are holding against yourself as a reason you can't live a life of extravagant love. Include past failures as well as current struggles. Offer them to God for his forgiveness, and then either burn your list or tear it into a hundred pieces, knowing "he forgives your sins—every one" (Psalm 103:3, *The Message*).

CHAPTER 9

Heart Skills

When Dave and I drove away from the church on our wedding day almost twenty years ago, I dreamed that we would spend the rest of our lives looking at sunsets and gazing into each other's eyes with perfect love and passionate affection. In between sunsets, I imagined I would clean our home until it sparkled like the ones in the Pine-Sol commercials while Dave worked in a job that he loved and where he was well-paid and appreciated. In my fantasy, he would be home by 5:15 P.M. and we would eat meals fit for the cover of *Bon Appetit*. After he did the dishes, we would read to one another from Shakespeare and Browning. Then we would have an in-depth Bible study followed by a time of prayer, after which Dave would gently lead me into the bedroom and we would make wild, passionate love.

Well…

Last night I rented a movie to watch with my husband. I purposefully chose a movie I thought he might enjoy. I struggled valiantly to stay awake through the movie, but I must have dozed off during part of the film because when it was over Dave asked, "Did you enjoy your little nap?" I know he asked this question innocently, perhaps even teasingly, but I reacted defensively. I retorted, "Can't you just appreciate when I try to do something for you?" And I stomped off to bed without even saying good night.

I woke up about 5:00 A.M. feeling ashamed of my childishness and sorry for going to sleep with an angry heart. I decided to get out of bed and try to work. I looked at my computer screen and imagined the words flashing across the screen in bright red letters: *You're Going to Write a Book About Relationships?!?!?!?*

My heart felt heavy and drained of energy. I turned off the computer and retreated to the chair in my office where I often pray and reflect. I confessed my sin from the night before, and I admitted my longings for my husband. I want him to know how much I love him, and I want him to be grateful and appreciate me! But when I don't get my way, I still want to be generous, kind, persistent, and forgiving.

I left my time of prayer and reflection with renewed resolve to love extravagantly. Without that time with God, I might have gone through this day with a curt and angry spirit and lived for an inferior or even destructive purpose. I might have silently determined to never rent a movie with Dave's interests in mind again. The day could have ended with halfhearted apologies from both of us, and we would have brushed this minor conflict under the carpet.

Instead, I fixed Dave's favorite breakfast and served it with a coupon for a movie night sometime during the next month. I confessed both my hurt and sin to him, and he apologized for not being attentive to my gift to him of the movie selection. My heart felt free.

A minor "paper cut" in our relationship? Yes. But allowed to go unattended, paper cuts can eventually drain the life out of our heart for relationships.

I entered marriage believing that a good relationship would happen naturally, that when you really love someone, everything works out. It didn't take me very long to realize that Dave and I were experiencing difficulties, conflicts, and disappointments—naturally. What's true of marriage is true of all relationships, be they with friends, children, coworkers, or family: Good relationships require work. Hard work. But it is work that we, as women, are uniquely equipped for because of the longings written in our hearts by our Creator.

Each day we can begin with a clear sense of purpose: We are created for relationships. And we can engage in this purpose with whole hearts as we examine our choices, confess our sins, and receive God's love and forgiveness. But what will all this look like in practical terms? In this chapter we will consider four practical skills that will enable us to love extravagantly.

Skills for loving well are developed through practice as we begin each day with a heart wholly dedicated to this purpose. One of the best expressions of extravagant love I know of comes from the story of Ruth. Consider Ruth's statement to Naomi at the beginning of their recorded experience in Scripture.

> Ruth replied, "Don't urge me to leave you or to turn back from you. Where you go I will go, and where you stay I will stay. Your people will be my people and your God my God. Where you die I will die, and there I will be buried. May the LORD deal with me, be it ever so severely, if anything but death separates you and me." (Ruth 1:16-17)

As you reflect on your relationships, consider making such a statement of purpose with regard to your spouse, friends, children, and family members. Does it seem a little extreme? Good. This commitment is the beginning of extravagant love.

Ruth's statement seems even more radical when you consider the object of her commitment. Naomi was not the most winsome friend at the time. Although both Naomi and Ruth had experienced staggering losses, Naomi cruelly distances herself from Ruth by saying, in essence, "I have suffered more than you" (1:13). Then she dismisses Ruth's request to go to Israel with her and practically orders her to stay in Moab: "Look, your sister-in-law is going back to her people and her gods. Go back with her" (1:15).

It is *after* Naomi's heartless and harsh words that Ruth makes her incredible statement of devotion. Didn't Ruth see the mean, bitter woman in front of her? The whole story of the book hinges on the fact that Ruth did not.

Seeing with Your Heart

The first skill necessary to loving with abandon is seeing with your heart. The only explanation for Ruth's statement and the incredible events that follow is that she was a woman who saw with her heart. Of course, she saw the empty, unkind, faithless woman in front of her. But she must have also seen a woman whose heart was full of love, grief, and longing, because she knew all too well the losses Naomi had experienced.

Ruth also saw a woman who must have been kind to her during the course of their relationship, and she remembered those kindnesses. Perhaps Naomi helped Ruth set up her household when she married Naomi's son. It's possible they shared chores and worked together closely. Because Naomi and her husband came to Moab as strangers to the community, leaving their families behind, it stands to reason that Naomi's closest friends were her daughters-in-law.

Ruth, no doubt, expressed her longing for children to her mother-in-law, and perhaps Naomi comforted her and suggested that they pray to Naomi's God. I am certain when Naomi carelessly suggested that she join Orpah, her other daughter-in-law, and go back to their false gods, Ruth must have shuddered. She knew of Naomi's faith, and that expression of faith over the course of their relationship undoubtedly compelled Ruth to leave her own homeland and religion and declare her commitment to Naomi and the God of Israel. Ruth saw with her heart what was *most true* about Naomi, that she was a woman full of compassion, kindness, and faith.

We've all had loved ones make unkind comments or unjust assumptions about us like Naomi did when she concluded her suffering was greater than Ruth's. And who hasn't had a spouse, child, or friend try to push us away like Naomi tried to push away Ruth? What keeps us from retreating from these relationships in hurt and disappointment and instead allows us to enter into extravagant love? Seeing with our hearts. And seeing with our hearts requires that we be detectives for dignity. We must be relentless in looking for the strengths, gifts, and abilities of the people God has placed in our lives.

A client of mine recently explained her despair about her fourteen-year-old daughter: "I am just sick of my daughter. She is so selfish and focused on material things. I just want to tell her to go to her room and get out of my sight." Having an adolescent daughter myself, I could empathize with the tumult that a teenager brings into the home, but I feared that if she expressed only these thoughts to her daughter, she might end up with a severed relationship and a daughter more bent on destruction than ever.

I asked her to tell me some stories from her daughter's childhood. She described a girl of wit, loyalty, and adventure, and then told me about her daughter's commitment to Christ as an eleven-year-old. I suggested that she creatively remind her daughter of some of those qualities. But she lamented, "That girl is gone. Those qualities don't show themselves any-more!"

I asked her to become a detective, looking for clues to the girl she knew was there, trapped in that adolescent body. I reminded her that she was up to the task because no one knew her daughter like she did (at this point, not even her daughter knew herself like her mother did), and no one loved her more fiercely.

· The next week my client came back and told me a delightful story. Her daughter had come home from school and stormed up to her room shouting, "I need to go shopping! I'm the only one in my class who doesn't have something to wear from Abercrombie & Fitch. It's so unfair. I hate my life!"

This brave mother gave her daughter a few minutes to cool off and then knocked on her door.

"Come in," her daughter snarled as only a teenage girl can.

"Do you want to go shopping?" the mom asked winsomely.

"Can we? Can we go to Abercrombie?" Her daughter was hopeful.

"I wish we could, but you know we don't have the money to buy what even one T-shirt would cost there. Why is having something from that store so important?"

"Everyone else does, and I feel like an outcast if I don't."

"I can see why that would make you so angry." Her mother surprised her with empathy. And then this wise mother reminded her daughter of a story from her childhood when a new girl had come to Sunday school and everyone had shunned her because she spoke with a lisp. Her daughter had not only befriended the new girl, but she led the rest of the class in accepting her. "You have always been a leader because of your loyalty and hatred for discrimination," she told her child.

"Well, now it's my turn to be discriminated against, and I can't take it anymore!"

Once again the mother looked past her daughter's adolescent dramatics and sympathized: "I can understand why you feel that way. Your friends are foolish if they are treating you differently because you don't have a shirt with the words *Abercrombie & Fitch* on it. You've always believed qualities like a sense of humor, a commitment to God, and the pursuit of goals are more important than clothes. You must be so disappointed in your friends."

After this she left the room, gently shut her daughter's door, and prayed that her daughter would remember the truth about herself, even in the midst of teenage insanity.

The next morning the daughter came down for breakfast dressed in an outfit that astounded her mother. She wore blue jeans and a gray T-shirt with neatly printed lettering across the back that read: *Kmart*. Her daughter explained, "I decided it's time to start a new trend. I talked Erin [her best friend] into doing it too!"

As the mother watched her incredibly spirited, adventurous, wonderful daughter leave for school, she prayed: "Lord, don't let me ever forget who she is. Give me eyes to see—really see."

Does seeing with the heart mean that we should close our eyes to sinful behavior? Of course not. As mothers we have an obligation to discipline and instruct our children and to be persistent in training them. But in our relationship with them, and in our relationships with our spouse or friends and other family members, a good rule of thumb is to look for nine positive qualities for every one negative quality we see. Perhaps you're thinking: "You don't know my friend/child/husband. There just aren't that many good things to see." Remember, extravagant love is hard work, and learning to see from your heart will be challenging. But your innate longings are a reliable compass as you attempt to steer your heart in the right direction.

This would be a good place for me to describe a resource that can help you in this difficult but invigorating work, and that is a relationship journal. In this notebook, dedicate a page to each person in your life that you are committed to loving extravagantly. Write down clues that you observe about who they are. Pray for God to give you eyes to truly see. You might want to write a few reminders to yourself in this journal:

- Let go of thinking this person will fulfill my every expectation.
- What do I enjoy about her (or him)?
- What do I desire for her?
- What have I experienced from her that does not seem to reflect who God created her to be?

Perhaps you're concerned that I'm minimizing sin and taking an "I'm OK, You're OK" approach. After all, what will happen if we don't always point out others' faults, sins, and weaknesses? Won't that only encourage them in their bad behavior?

This is the most freeing part about extravagant love: It is not our job to save people. That is God's job. He promises: "[I am] not willing that any should perish, but that all should come to repentance" (2 Peter 3:9, KJV). Seeing with your heart requires faith that God can be trusted with the people in your life. Your primary work is to be who God created you to be: a woman full of longing for relationship, kindness, wisdom, insight, purpose—all components of extravagant love.

I realize that for some of you this might be a bigger job than for others due to the difficult people in your life, and I don't want to minimize the heartaches or complications you are experiencing. You may need to seek counsel, to find a support group, or even to separate from a relationship that is destructive. But also keep in mind that there are an infinite number of ways to pray again, try again, and risk again in relationships. When we do what needs to be done for love, we shine with dignity. When I meet women who courageously love in the midst of incredibly difficult circumstances, I am filled with respect for them and reminded of God's unique design of women to be both tender and strong.

SPEAKING FROM YOUR HEART

Naomi's response to Ruth's extravagant devotion is a bit disappointing. As they enter Naomi's hometown, the entire community gathers around them, brimming with curiosity. You might imagine Naomi's introduction would go something like this: "Yes, I have returned due to great loss, but I am so grateful to be able to introduce my daughter-in-law. Ruth has supported me and stood by me and offered me comfort and companionship even in the midst of her own loss. Please welcome her."

Naomi's response is quite different: "Don't call me Naomi," she told them. "Call me Mara, because the Almighty has made my life very bitter. I went away full, but the LORD has brought me back empty" (1:20-21).

Can you imagine how Naomi's words stung? Ruth must have winced at Naomi's complete disregard of her. Aren't you curious to know what Ruth's first recorded words to Naomi are after this dismal introduction? It's about time for Ruth to confront Naomi and point out her cruelty, bitterness, and lack of faith!

Instead, Ruth makes a request: "Let me go to the fields and pick up the leftover grain behind anyone in whose eyes I find favor" (2:2). She asks Naomi how she can be of help! She offers to give of herself, even though Naomi was not particularly lovely or deserving at the moment. On the strength of her commitment alone, Ruth surveys the state of their relationship and asks, "What can I do?"

Extravagant love speaks from the heart. Thoughtful feminists write about the silence of women and the depression that often follows when women do not feel free to express themselves. I agree with them. Many feminists, however, blame a patriarchal culture for the silencing of women. This is where I disagree. We are silent because we do not understand the nature of real love.

Extravagant love compels women to speak the truth in love. But we are sometimes confused about how and when to speak the truth. There are three guiding principles for speaking the truth in love: (1) Pay attention to yourself, (2) pray about timing, and (3) practice without words.

Pay Attention to Yourself

As you record data in your relationship journal, follow Ruth's example. The first and most important question to ask in the midst of a struggling or growing relationship is "What can I do?" You can change your relationships by first changing yourself. As you pray about the disappointments your loved one has caused, what are their behaviors telling you about yourself?

A very important and freeing principle of extravagant love is that you cannot change another person. That's God's work. You cannot force your friends, children, or spouse to act in certain ways. Punishing, withdrawing, or trying to make people do what you want almost always backfires and inevitably turns you into the woman you do not want to be. When Ruth remembered her commitment and accepted the challenge to work on herself first, she set out on a course that would transform a woman from Moab into the great-grandmother of Israel's most famous king…and part of the lineage of Christ, the King of kings!

Pray About Timing

Speaking the truth in love does require saying hard things. I do not know a formula to explain how and when to confront a loved one about difficult matters. Listening to your own heart and seeking God's heart on the matter will look different for everyone. But before speaking, you do need to ask yourself if you are willing to be vulnerable. Your words cannot be designed as walls to shut people out. Walls, after all, serve more to imprison you than to keep others out. When you're vulnerable, you have nothing to defend. When you're vulnerable, you let go of pride and self-righteousness because you've looked honestly at the "plank" in your own eye before confronting your loved one about the "speck" in his (Matthew 7:3-5).

Our family had a reunion this past year. One of my brothers behaved in a way that embarrassed my mother and hurt both of my parents deeply. My mom considered writing him a letter and rebuking him for his thoughtless actions. But after much prayer and reflection, she decided to wait. She knew if she wrote, it would be out of hurt and anger. She suspected he wouldn't respond well, and the walls between them would become even thicker.

Months after the reunion my mom wrote a letter to my brother disclosing her growing fear that as she and my father approached old age they would not have a close relationship with my brother. She asked if there was anything she could do to help their relationship. Her words were vulnerable, kind, and filled with longing. In between the lines were the memories of the disappointing events at the reunion.

My brother has not yet responded to the letter, but my mother is unashamed of her heart for her son. She trusts that God will take her words and "catch" her wayward child.

Speaking the truth in love does not guarantee the results we want in the people we love, but we are promised the rewards of loving extravagantly in our own lives as we are "being transformed into his likeness with ever-increasing glory" (2 Corinthians 3:18). And during this transformation, we have fellowship with the One who is the Word incarnate:

> He came to his own people,
>   but they didn't want him.
> But whoever did want him…
> These are the God-begotten….

The Word became flesh and blood,
>   and moved into the neighborhood.
We saw the glory with our own eyes…
Generous inside and out,
>   true from start to finish. (John 1:11-14, *The Message*)

What a wonderful model of speaking words of life and bringing love to life, even when we do not always receive the response we long for. "We all live off his generous bounty, gift after gift after gift" (1:16)!

Practice Without Words

We've focused a lot on the demands of extravagant love, but practicing it can be great fun as well. In your relationship journal, keep a growing list of ways to say, "I love you." Here are some ideas to get you started:

- Hang mistletoe in your house year-round!
- Create a time capsule for each of your children, to be opened at graduation.
- Once a week for a year write down qualities you love about your friend, spouse, mom, child, and then give him or her the list.
- Take dancing lessons together.
- Learn to cook. (This one may apply only to me!)
- Write letters to your children and mail them. Everyone loves to get mail.
- Send flowers to a friend for no reason.
- Cover up all clocks in your house for the weekend and see what happens when you're not constrained by time.
- Create a holiday: Friend Appreciation Day.

I have a friend who told me about his grandmother's extravagant and delightful expression of love. My friend entered adolescence confused and angry. At the age of thirteen he decided that the ultimate rebellion, the final act to alienate himself from his family, would be to pierce his ear and wear an earring. The earring had the desired effect on his parents and church, affirming his decision to run away from home.

He made one stop on his way out: his grandmother's house. His grandmother took one look at the earring and pulled out her jewelry box, suggesting he wear solid gold instead of imitation!

Practicing extravagant love without using words can help make you more aware of the moment-by-moment choices you are making in a relationship. No choice is too small to make a difference. One of the most amazing payoffs of developing your creativity in this area is that you will become more aware of the delightful and diverse ways that God says, "I love you" to *you* every day. One of my daily prayers is, "Lord, don't let me fall asleep tonight without noting one of the ways you expressed your love to me today."

WEARING YOUR HEART ON YOUR SLEEVE

I'm not sure where this expression comes from, but it's not usually thought of as a flattering description. We live in a culture that instructs us to play it safe. From the time we're teenagers, we're conditioned not to be too enthusiastic or excited about anything. I have overheard my daughter and her friends remind each other that if a boy is interested in them, to not appear too eager or delighted by the attention. They don't think "being delighted" is cool. Even in committed relationships, it's all too easy to become indifferent or reserved.

But the heart set free to love extravagantly can't help but express itself! It is unselfconscious. After Ruth meets Boaz in the threshing field, she never once pretends that the unfolding story is no big deal. Just as her commitment to Naomi was unabashed and unashamed, her desire for Boaz's redemptive participation in her life was equally straightforward.

How did she dare to risk so radically? I can't be sure of the answer, but I agree with Pastor Jack Hayford who writes: "Make no mistake, this was an enormous decision for this young woman. Yet there was one thing. She had heard her husband and his family talk about a God in Israel. A God who had a famous name. A powerful God. A holy God. A God who shielded and delivered His people again and again."[1]

Ruth's story concludes with an incredible plan that results in Boaz redeeming Ruth and Naomi from poverty and despair, but it cannot be overlooked that this wonderful ending would not have happened without Ruth's unwavering and extravagant commitment to relationship.

When we don't wear our hearts on our sleeves, we hide them, believing we have good reason. To disclose and express our desires might mean rejection or disappointment. Every time I speak about extravagant love, someone will ask me, "If I live this way and announce to all the world my longings for love, I will make a fool of myself." After all, not every story ends like Ruth's.

Extravagant love is only possible to the degree that I am awash in God's lavish love. I am reminded of the story of the Jesuit retreat leader who pointed to the crucifix and remarked, "What a strange way to run the universe." Those whose love takes extravagant and sometimes embarrassing forms are those who believe that the crucified one shows the way because, in the words of Brennan Manning, "he came to us not with the crushing impact of unbearable glory but in the way of weakness, vulnerability, and need. Jesus was a naked, humiliated, exposed God on the cross who allowed us to get close to him."[2]

An elderly couple came to see me for counseling not long ago. Their visit, in and of itself, revealed to me that this was an extraordinary couple.

After all, it seems that as we get older, we usually become less vulnerable, more set in our ways, and more convinced that we can never change. But one of my friends who is a ski instructor told me about a sixty-five-year-old woman who decided to take skiing lessons. He described her slow descent down the mountain in the beginning snowplow position and told me that he thought of her as an "extreme skier," as courageous and adventurous as any daredevil skier. So when Harry and Esther told me they needed help improving their marriage, I thought of them as "extreme lovers."

I will never forget the counseling session in which Esther told me she thought their marriage was really changing and becoming the relationship they had always longed for. When Esther was thirty-seven years old, she learned that she had breast cancer and underwent a radical double mastectomy. She did not receive the support and counsel that is available to women today who have breast cancer. Reconstructive surgery was not even presented as an option.

Esther told me that she and Harry had never discussed the cancer or the surgery and that he had never even seen her scars. Esther understood that she had closed her heart to Harry during this agonizing time and that Harry had not pursued her. Esther courageously decided to disclose herself fully to Harry. As she allowed Harry to see her scars, she bravely "wore her heart on her sleeve," and they wept together, forgave one another, and began to talk about forty years of unspoken pain, fear, and longing. Esther is an extravagant lover of heroic proportions!

SACRIFICING FOR YOUR HEART

Not only does extravagant love transform us into the image of Christ and allow us to participate in the fellowship of his sufferings, it is good for us!

In his book *Love and Survival: Eight Pathways to Intimacy and Health,* Dr. Dean Ornish explained that on the most practical level, scientific studies indicate that people who are available for "deep emotional relationships live longer, have less heart disease and stomach problems." He continued,

> Put in another way, anything that promotes love is healing; anything that promotes isolation, separation, loneliness, loss, hostility, anger, cynicism, alienation, and related feelings leads to suffering, disease, and premature death from all causes. Most scientific studies have demonstrated the extraordinarily powerful role of love and relationships in determining health and illness.[3]

You can't get a more tangible payoff than that!

But even more important, I believe, no one can live with extravagant love and remain unchanged. Unfortunately, as Christian women we have often believed that means if we love, submit, honor, obey, and sacrifice, our loved ones will change. I wish I could tell you that if you see with your heart and become a detective *par excellence*, that if you speak from your heart the truth in love, and that if you wear your heart on your sleeve announcing your love and good intentions to all, the people around you will change and you will experience all that you long for. But it doesn't always happen that way. You may suffer, your loved ones may not change, you may fail, others may fail you. But *you* will change. Loving extravagantly transforms *you!*

One of my favorite people is a woman whose name is Tena. Tena came to me for counseling because she didn't know if she could stay in her marriage. It had been nineteen years of unbearable disappointment. She explained that one indication of their troubled marriage was that her husband had never given her a gift and gave her only one card that read, "Happy Birthday to a Great Guy!"

Tena had given up. She wanted out of the marriage. After several months of counseling, Tena admitted she no longer expected or looked for anything good in her husband, she never expressed anything personal to him, and he had no idea that she was thinking about leaving. I asked her if she would consider disclosing a few simple truths to her husband about her own heart, telling him that she was discouraged, hurt, and didn't know how much longer she could continue in their marriage as it was. She replied with a sentence I will never forget, "Why, that would be like my handing him a sword and asking him to finish me off."

I couldn't disagree with her. I asked her if it was a sacrifice she was willing to make. Now I need to say a word about sacrifice. I hope you know by now that I don't recommend being a doormat, zipping your mouth shut, and never paying attention to your own needs. Sadly, many of the sacrifices we make are for nothing. They are not prayerful, purposeful, and intentional sacrifices for the sake of giving others an opportunity to choose life.

For example, we may choose to remain silent to avoid conflict or so that people will like us. One woman told me about her choice to remain silent while her friend made negative and cynical comments about others. The comments drained their relationship of joy, but she didn't say anything because she didn't want to upset her friend or appear too sensitive. Finally, after many sleepless nights, she confronted her friend and was surprised by her receptive heart and request for help. We shortchange others in relationships when we just give scraps of ourselves.

Other times we make unwise sacrifices because we have become comfortable in the role of victim. We may allow people to hurt or disregard us and then secretly nurse our wounds. Once again, thoughtful feminists chastise women for sacrificing themselves and implore women to speak out so they no longer lose themselves. I agree with the feminists that a sacrifice for nothing is foolish at best and a misguided attempt for sainthood at worst. Extravagant love compels us to speak up, risking sacrifice, but sacrifice that will be for something while we trust the One who promises: "Whoever loses [her] life for my sake will find it" (Matthew 10:39).

Tena prayerfully and intentionally handed her husband the sword. He said to her, "Well, what do you want me to do?" She hadn't anticipated a response even slightly that vulnerable, but she quickly answered, "Come to marriage counseling with me."

To make a long story short, he agreed, although he wore his sunglasses during the entire hour of the first session! Tena and her husband have worked to change their marriage directly as a result of Tena's courageous choices to love extravagantly. Although Tena's husband has changed, the most dramatic change has been in Tena. She's been transformed from a bitter, brooding, despairing woman to a generous, joking, hopeful woman. Her marriage is far from perfect, and there is a lot of work still to be done, but for her last birthday she received twenty birthday cards from her husband—one for every year he'd missed!

Seeing with your heart, speaking from your heart, wearing your heart on your sleeve, and sacrificing for your heart will transform you into an extravagant lover. Hard work? Absolutely. But when you're an old woman at the end of your life and you evaluate your time on earth, I believe that there is only one question—beyond that of your salvation—that will really matter: *Did I love well?*

In the next chapter we will further explore what sustains us in the hard work of loving well. The courage to live a life of love is discovered as we determine to settle for nothing less.

LIVING IN LOVE

For Personal Reflection or Discussion

1. In the midst of difficult relationships, have you lost sight of what is *most true* about yourself or others? If so, how might your current perspective need to change?

2. When you consider the people in your life, do you most often look for clues to confirm something negative or something positive about them? Which focus have you chosen over the past twenty-four hours?

3. What are you afraid will happen in relationships if you don't vigilantly point out what people are doing wrong?

4. When was the last time you expressed delight in a relationship?

5. When did you last allow someone to see your "scars"?

Into Action

1. Take note of how you respond in relationships when things don't go the way you'd hoped or planned. Throughout the week ahead, write down disappointing scenarios and how you responded.

2. Begin a relationship journal as described in this chapter.

3. Make your own list of ideas for loving without words.

CHAPTER 10

Sustaining Your Heart

"I *can* love extravagantly," she said to me with a twinkle in her eye. "For about one week." Then the light in her eyes faded, and she challenged me: "Let's get real. Loving extravagantly is what I want, but it is not possible to sustain in the midst of difficult relationships or daily responsibilities."

My friend was expressing sentiments that we've all felt. How many times have we read a challenging book, heard a moving sermon, or attended a weekend retreat and determined to live and love differently, only to find that we're back in the same old patterns of living within a matter of days or weeks?

When I talk with women about relationships, I discover we share two commonalities of the heart: (1) We long for extravagant love, and (2) we get discouraged easily. Discouragement usually comes when we're reminded that the people in our lives aren't always easy to love, appreciative of our efforts, or changing like we thought they might. Discouragement takes hold when we begin to ask: "Why do I always have to be the one to do the work? I'm always the one who calls, initiates, and pursues. I'm tired of being responsible."

From the moment we are born, the Enemy, the fallen world, and our own need to be safe conspire to distort and destroy our sacred longing for relationships. Proverbs reminds us that if we want our hearts to gush with wellsprings of life, we must guard them (4:23). The warning from Thomas à Kempis, the author of *The Imitation of Christ*, further underscores how important it is to protect our hearts: "Know well that the Enemy laboureth in all wise to kill thy desire in good and to make thee void of all good exercise."

So what does it mean to guard our hearts in order to sustain growth and live a life of lavish love, even when the landscape around us is parched and dry? Well, hard work, for starters. Extravagant love is hard work.

I don't know about you, but the news that a life of love is hard came as a mixed message to me. On one hand, I was relieved. No wonder I was struggling, straining, and groaning in the exercises of extravagance! It wasn't supposed to be easy. But on the other hand, I was discouraged. I wanted to believe that I could find a formula or methodology that would enable me to love effortlessly.

A lot of my counseling is with women who struggle with addictions, so I was intrigued to learn that there is a new form of treatment for those who want to break free from substance dependency. Addicts who can afford to pay their own medical costs (usually $3,500 to $6,000) simply check into the hospital or a specialized clinic for what is called "rapid detox." The addict is "out" for six to eight hours and is pumped full of fluids and medications that allow the body to detoxify. The patient awakens with no drugs or alcohol in her system and with none of the harrowing symptoms of withdrawal. Presto. Chango.

The downside of rapid detox, opponents argue, is that it's too easy. It is the memories of the bad experiences of withdrawal as well as the persistent work of recovery that prevent relapse. But I must admit it still sounded pretty good to me. I mean, why must change require so much work?

You Must Participate in Your Own Rescue

My answer came when I was in a raft on the Arkansas River last summer. Our family adventured out one Saturday in May for what I thought would be a fun, relaxing float down the river.

"Listen up!" the guide began. "I need to give you a few safety precautions." He proceeded to outline all of the dangers that might await us on the ten-mile stretch of whitewater, as well as their remedies. I strained to pay attention, but all the perilous possibilities left me wondering if I could even remember which was upstream and which was downstream. The guide, who looked to be all of twenty, explained that if we fell into the river, when we caught our breath from the shock of the forty-degree water, we should look for him to indicate if we should swim or float on our backs in the "river position." He stressed: "You must participate in your own rescue."

"Any questions?" asked our guide, who asked us to call him "Ax." I wanted to ask him how often people fell out of the boat, but when I raised my hand my children gave me The Look that said, "Please don't embarrass us by acting too old," so I forced a smile and said: "Never mind, Ax."

We carried the raft to the river's edge and got into place. The shock of the icy water made me gasp.

"Everything okay up there?" Ax called out.

"No problem," I replied with forced confidence. Maybe I *was* too old.

"We've got about five miles before we hit the canyon with the rapids, so let's practice our paddle stroke," Ax cheerily suggested. It quickly became apparent that my paddling would only interfere with the progress of our raft, so Ax suggested that I just enjoy the ride and leave all the paddling to him.

"No problem," I said again. I'll just place my life in the hands of someone whose name is a tool (or a murder weapon) and who lives in a tent.

"Here we go-o-o-o-o," Ax interrupted my contemplative terror. "We start with a small one—a Level Two rapid. Let's ride it!"

I held on for dear life. The cold water splashed right through the openings in my life jacket, jolting me to attention. I remained securely seated on the side of the raft though. No problem. I relaxed a little.

"There she is!" Ax shouted jubilantly. "The 'Widow-maker.' This is a Level Four rapid. You are going to get wet!"

The hilarity in his voice scared me. I stared at the six-foot wall of water heading right for us. The boat dropped and, without thinking, I reached for my son. My motherly instinct propelled me to protect him (he was fine, of course, without me) and moved me out of my secure position in the raft. I bounced backward into the rushing water and was engulfed with a shock of cold. I felt myself simultaneously pulled into the current and locked in the grip of the icy water. I struggled to raise my head above the water, swallowing the river and choking it back up at the same time. I couldn't remember what I was supposed to do. It didn't matter. I was going to drown, and my children would never forgive me.

My mind flashed back to the safety talk, and I remembered Ax's smiling, suntanned face: "You must participate in your own rescue." I struggled to find the boat. Ax was motioning to me. He was telling me to swim. Now I had a new worry. I wasn't sure I could remember how to swim. And all of a sudden I was six years old again, shivering in the shallow end of our neighborhood swimming pool. My mother had signed me up for swimming lessons, and I attended faithfully every chilly morning for two weeks. At the end of the two weeks, we had to swim the length of the pool. I stuck my face in the cold water and began the motions we practiced daily: reach, breathe, kick; reach, breathe, kick.

"Grab the paddle. Just reach out and grab it!" Ax shouted. I was no longer in the safe boundaries of the neighborhood pool. I was in the white-water of the Arkansas River, reaching for the yellow paddle Ax was holding out to me, participating in my own rescue.

The rest of the river ride is a blur. I sat in the middle of the boat, shivering uncontrollably, and praying for the ride to end quickly. I remembered reading that a cubic foot of water weighs about sixty-two pounds. I shuddered with relief to be free from the weight of all that freezing, churning water.

In the car on the way home, I couldn't stop thinking about my near drowning and the story of the parting of the Red Sea. I wondered at the weight of all that water and the ease with which God parted it to deliver the Israelites from bondage. The miracle is so compelling that I had always focused on God's part and had not thought much about the required participation from the Israelites. Did they quake with terror for their children as the walls of water rose on either side of them? How did they fight off their fears and keep moving through the strange tunnel of water? And when they finally reached the other side, how could they ever forget this dumbfounding deliverance? Surely the sight of the parting sea, the feel of the dry land beneath their feet, and the sound of Egyptian soldiers and horses drowning behind them would be etched forever in their hearts and minds.

That is the kind of deliverance I long for—the kind that changes everything forever. The deliverance I experience, however, seems more murky than miraculous, more daily than dramatic. It's deliverance made up of arms and legs tired and sore from exercise.

When we got home from our waterlogged adventure, I found my Bible and reread the story of the Israelites' miraculous delivery. Sure enough, it was all there just as I remembered it. I read on in the story and stopped, stunned: Only three days after deliverance, the Israelites were ready to go back into slavery because they couldn't find drinking water. "Didn't we say to you in Egypt, 'Leave us alone…?' It would have been better for us to serve the Egyptians than to die in the desert" (Exodus 14:12). They didn't even mention the Red Sea!

My afternoon on the Arkansas and my memory of all those swimming lessons came to mind. I wondered if the miracle at the Red Sea was too rapid and too dramatic to etch memories strong and deep enough to carry the Israelites all the way to the Promised Land. God gave the Israelites forty more years of struggle to weave together God's works and their own works into a tapestry of deliverance.

We must participate in our own rescue. We get tired, feel alone, and don't want to be responsible any longer, and yet God says, "Let us not become weary in doing good, for at the proper time we will reap a harvest if we do not give up" (Galatians 6:9).

Why does God require that we exercise to sustain extravagant love? The apostle Paul answers: "Be energetic in your life of salvation, reverent and sensitive before God. That energy is *God's* energy, an energy deep within you, God himself willing and working at what will give him the most pleasure" (Philippians 2:12-13, *The Message*). What a mystery! When we work, we experience God and he energizes us. Nothing brings him more pleasure and brings us more reward.

In his excellent, challenging book *The Spirit of the Disciplines,* Dallas Willard encourages: "The Spirit of the Disciplines is nothing but the love of Jesus, with its resolute will to be like him whom we love. In the fellowship of the burning heart, 'exercise unto godliness' is our way of receiving ever more fully the grace in which we stand, rejoicing in the hope of the glory of God (Romans 5:2)."[1]

In chapter 6, we discussed four hallmarks of destructive relationships that rob our hearts of the energy for extravagant love: unhealthy habits, compulsive behavior, secret satisfaction, and isolating choices. In order to guard our hearts so they remain free for extravagant love, we must practice four exercises that are the antitheses of the choices that entangle us in destructive relationships: discipline, surrender, transparency, and connection.

THE DISCIPLINED HEART

Discipline is the cornerstone of extravagant love. One of the reasons that discipline sometimes seems like drudgery is that we don't elevate it to its proper position. Discipline can actually become a joy when you take the time to create your own sacred space in which to practice your disciplines—a space where you can ensure your privacy, enjoy your surroundings, and nourish your spiritual life. Such a space can become a blessed refuge where your heart can be nurtured and sustained for your life of extravagant love.

My sacred space is my office. On one wall I have photographs of many of the meaningful people in my life. My office is filled with all the books I love. I often light candles and put fresh flowers on my desk. A sacred space should be much like the tea party described in Elizabeth Berg's novel *The Pull of the Moon*:

> I remember once seeing a tea party set up with mismatched china,
> decorations of a plucked pansy blossom and a seashell and shiny
> penny and a small circle of red berries and a fern, pressed wetly
> into the wooden table, the damp outline a beautiful bonus. They
> didn't consult the Martha Stewart guide for entertainment. They

pulled ideas from their hearts and minds about the things that gave them pleasure, and they laid out an offering with loving intent. It was a small Garden of Eden, the occupants making something out of what they saw. Out of what they truly saw.[2]

What a concept! For discipline to be a practice lovingly prepared and intentionally chosen. The capacity to love extravagantly in moments of tedium or crisis rests uniquely and essentially upon the depths of a wise and rigorous practice of disciplines of the heart: listening, examining, confessing, meditating, praying, and studying and worshiping.

Listening

When you reserve time for yourself in practiced quietness, you can stay connected with your heart full of longings for relationships by remembering your past, looking for God in your present, and dreaming about your future. You won't be as prone to forget what you were made for and slide into living for lesser purposes.

Part of listening to your heart is developing your "muscles" of self-esteem. Are you regularly taking inventory of your talents, strengths, eccentricities, resources, and passions?

Examining

Are your relationships unsatisfactory, boring, hurtful, disappointing? Then pay close attention to yourself. Where do you spend your heart's energy?

Confessing

Be attentive to moments of truth when you are "caught" in misdirecting the energy of your heart. Welcome the opportunity to bow in repentance before the One who offers forgiveness and freedom.

Meditating

Putting yourself in God's stories and placing God in your own story inevitably results in a posture of gratitude. Gratitude opens your heart to receive blessings.

Praying

Prayer heals the broken heart. I'm convinced that it's not what we say, but the act of laying out our hearts before God that makes prayer a powerful agent of healing. I take great comfort in these words:

> Meanwhile, the moment we get tired in the waiting, God's Spirit is right alongside helping us along. If we don't know how or what to pray, it doesn't matter. He does our praying in and for us, making prayer out of our wordless sighs, our aching groans. He knows us far better than we know ourselves, knows our pregnant condition, and keeps us present before God. That's why we can be so sure that every detail in our lives of love for God is worked into something good. (Romans 8:26-28, *The Message*)

Studying and Worshiping

Engage yourself in the written word. As women, I don't think anything frustrates or discourages us more in relationships than passivity. We echo God's heart when he grieves: "I know you inside and out, and find little to my liking. You're not cold, you're not hot—far better to be either cold or hot! You're stale. You're stagnant" (Revelation 3:15, *The Message*). Intimate relationship with God is not possible as long as we are passive. Cultivating a relationship requires that we contribute, and one way to do that is through study. You may have noted that I've quoted many scriptures from *The Message*, Eugene Peterson's translation of the Bible into contemporary English.

When I'm particularly tired or discouraged, I find reading from this translation nourishing and encouraging.

Of course, the passion of God's love for us never cools. But still, a one-sided love affair isn't very satisfactory. We engage in this love affair when we worship. Worship is to actively recognize God as worthy. In worship, God himself meets us. Worship fills our hearts and minds with wonder of him. True worship is a gift—a gift that is initiated as God, through his Spirit, reveals to us a glimpse of who he is. How can we get a glimpse of God and remain passive? Worship is encountering One who is beyond words, One who for that moment surrounds and fills our every longing and empty place. As we respond, he enters in and meets us. We feel his pleasure, and it becomes ours. Worship is what we were created for. But once again, worship requires practice, effort, and daily exercise.

Entire books have been written about each of the disciplines mentioned in this section, and I encourage you to read to broaden your understanding of these practices, so essential to sustaining your heart for extravagant love. Prepare, practice, and participate in your own rescue.

THE SURRENDERED HEART

Surrender is all about hope. Hope is an expectation of receiving, a conviction that there is a way to obtain what we long for. Where we place our hope determines what we surrender to. We were made to surrender to someone or something. Sadly, in our holy hunger for relationships we often surrender to unholy gods.

I wish that you all could meet my friend Pam. She has taught me much about the surrendered heart through her own life of surrender. Shortly after she got married almost thirty years ago, she received her graduate degree in child development and began teaching elementary school. She had her life all figured out. She believed that if she worked hard and did everything well, she would have the job, marriage, and family she longed for. Her hope was in her good works and competency.

Pam laughs now as she talks about what a good teacher she was to her students, but what an uncompassionate partner she was to the parents. During parent-teacher conferences, she had all the answers. As a mother with grown children now, she cringes at her self-righteous confidence then. She suspects that the Godhead met for a conference of their own to discuss Pam and lovingly determined, "We've got to stop her."

Pam and her husband were unbelievers when they met and married. While Pam was teaching, a fellow teacher faithfully presented the gospel to Pam and broke to her both the bad and good news. You can imagine how Pam's hopes were crushed when she learned that the message of the gospel begins with the news that you can never be good enough. Pam struggled with letting go of her false hope for several weeks before she accepted the work of Christ as payment for her sin and his righteousness as her strength and covering for now and for eternity.

After Pam accepted Christ, she fully expected that her husband would join her in her newfound faith. That was twenty-eight years ago, and her husband is still an unbeliever. God has not kept pace with Pam's agenda.

About ten years after Pam became a Christian, after many sleepless nights and agonizing struggles, Pam learned that her oldest son had a learning disability. If she could, Pam would tell you about all the months and years she spent learning to let her son be who God made him to be, not who she planned and hoped he would be. Slowly and gently, God was pulling Pam's hopes for the perfect marriage and family out from under her.

Fortunately, her false hopes gave way to surrender. Surrender to what?

An unbelieving husband and a struggling son? No. Surrender to the freeing truth that God is God and she is not. And from that truth, surrender to a loving, wise, and trustworthy heavenly Father.

When Pam decided to trust God with her son, she began to love him with a lighter heart and looser grip. When he was in the sixth grade, she began to meet with him once a week at the place of his choice (at that time it was Burger King) to hear about his struggles in school and his ideas for easing his load. They did a Bible study together, talked about girls, and commiserated about the incomprehensible "rules" for learning to spell. To this day, Pam and her son continue their meetings, although he is now a young adult and his tastes in restaurants have gotten much more expensive!

Pam's husband would tell you that he has the utmost respect for his wife's faith and that he watches her and asks her questions continually. Through their struggle with their son, Pam's husband watched her faith grow and mature amidst the imperfections of their life. He recently joined Pam in a couple's Bible study, and they are planning a trip to Israel together. Pam's continual prayers for her husband and her creative, intentional choices about their spiritual life together challenge me in my own marriage to plan for and pray about our spiritual interactions.

But what is most compelling about Pam's life is her daily walk with God. Pam's story of hoping, waiting, praying, trying, succeeding, failing, hurting, and enjoying has taught her that the most intimate relationship is available with God as she surrenders to him. In her life I see the fruit of a surrendered heart. I could tell you about the lonely truck driver (a woman) she led to Christ; the friend with cancer she powerfully comforted; the couple with a troubled son she guided through dark, stormy days; and the friend (me!) she relentlessly encouraged to go back to graduate school, get her degree in counseling, and someday put pen to paper in fulfilling her dream of writing a book.

Today Pam's life is relationally rich, not because of her competence and ability to make things "work," but because of her honest struggles and her powerful hope in God.

Two years ago I attended her fiftieth birthday party with women from all around the country who traveled to Colorado for the event. Pam shared the song of her heart from the book of Romans:

> There's more to come: We continue to shout our praise even when we're hemmed in with troubles, because we know how troubles can develop passionate patience in us, and how that patience in turn forges the tempered steel of virtue, keeping us alert for whatever God will do next. In alert expectancy such as this, we're never left feeling shortchanged. Quite the contrary—we can't round up enough containers to hold everything God generously pours into our lives through the Holy Spirit! (Romans 5:3-5, *The Message*)

That's the song of Pam's heart. What is the song of *your* heart? In the course of your life of love, you will need to continually evaluate where you place your hope. You'll know your hope is in a false god when the inevitable danger, disappointment, and struggle of relationships cause you to despair and consider quitting. When you are confronted with the disappointments of relationships, you can exercise hope by prayerfully reminding yourself: "Whom have I in heaven but you? And earth has nothing I desire besides you. My flesh and my heart may fail, but God is the strength [the hope] of my heart and my portion forever" (Psalm 73:25-26).

Daily, hourly surrender is an exercise that frees the heart for extravagance. Your place of surrender may be with a husband who's not talkative, a daughter who's not neat, a friend who's forgetful, or a family member who doesn't share your faith.

For years I harbored anger and resentment toward my husband because he never planned fun family events. He always paid for, participated in, and supported me in the planning, but I'd always hoped for a husband who would sweep me off my feet by planning special treats.

A few years ago, I became convicted about my bitter spirit and asked God's forgiveness as well as Dave's. I surrendered my need for a planning husband to God and *his* plans for me. Dave explained that he never planned because he felt certain he could never do a good enough job. How could he compete with the Queen of Planning? He also explained that he knew I wanted him to be different, better at something that he felt unequipped for (he grew up in a family that never celebrated). He vulnerably disclosed to me the hurt of knowing that I wanted him to be someone he was not.

My heart broke over my cruelty toward him. There is no greater damage we do to the people we love than by perverting our hope into wishing they were someone else. Since our conversation, Dave has planned some wonderful family times. But I learned an important lesson: When Dave disappoints me, I am in a perfect place to surrender to God.

When we do not surrender our hearts to God, not only do we miss an opportunity to develop and deepen intimacy with him, but we also charge ahead into relationships with an angry and hardened heart that will inflict hurt rather than with a soft and transparent heart that invites intimacy.

THE TRANSPARENT HEART

Disclosing our hearts to each other may bring pain and even involve danger—the risk of being wounded by someone we love. Indeed, to be involved in *any* relationship is to be both healed and hurt. Our choice is not over whether we will be healed or hurt, but rather to which of these inevitable experiences we will direct our focus.

When a beautiful young woman tells me, in almost a whisper, that she is drinking three to four glasses of wine every night to relax from the pressures of her upwardly mobile life, she expects a lecture and is surprised to see tears stream down my face. I tell her about a young woman who made similar choices and felt hopelessly trapped and found freedom—and together we believe that there is hope for her, too. For a moment I want to forget my shameful choices and the harm they caused me and others. But in doing so, I also remove myself from the forgiveness, strength, and joy I discovered in the process of healing.

Disclosure is powerful, both for the speaker and the listener. Often, it is in telling another the truth about ourselves that we discover the truth more fully. Sixteenth-century poet John of the Cross warns about the consequences of not being transparent: "The virtuous soul that is alone and without witnesses is like a burning coal. It will grow colder rather than hotter."

Transparency is life-giving, but we all know it can also open the door to negative or hurtful experiences. That's why I love the story of Ruth and Naomi. For me it is a picture of what so often heals the hurt of relationships, and that is simply *staying in relationships*. Ruth's commitment to Naomi redeemed the emptiness Naomi described at the beginning of the story, and it resulted in redemption for Ruth as well. The women of the community said to Naomi: "Praise be to the LORD, who this day has not left you without a kinsman-redeemer.... For your daughter-in-law, who loves you and who is better to you than seven sons, has given him birth" (Ruth 4:14-15). Through Ruth, God redeemed Naomi's barrenness.

The transparent heart expresses need, disappointment, satisfaction, and joy, and the transparent heart *hangs in there*. The combination of being vulnerable and remaining committed sustains us to love extravagantly. As we continue to practice transparency even when the going gets rough, we learn that we are related to each other through need, through sweat and tears—that we are connected by the holy longing for relationships written into our hearts.

THE CONNECTED HEART

The practices of being transparent and connecting with people are inevitably linked. Being involved with others and learning to take risks with them is essential in sustaining our hearts for extravagant love. We can learn to love extravagantly, but we cannot do it alone.

Are there women you talk with and pray with every week? Are you involved in Bible study, a book club, or a small group where you can share your story and join in the stories of others? I know getting involved can be awkward at first, and sometimes it seems that it's not getting you anywhere, just like all exercises when we're just getting started. But connecting with others is the only way to practice loving extravagantly.

Several weeks ago I ran into a friend I hadn't seen for some time. She had always struggled in her marriage, believing that since her husband was a perfectionist, she could never live up to his standards. She vacillated between self-pity and anger, and it seemed their marriage was always in tumult. When I asked her how things were going, she surprised me with her response: "Really well." She explained that she and her husband continue to struggle with the same old issues, but she thinks they're handling the struggles with more grace and maturity. I asked her what had brought about the change, and she replied, "I guess we're finally accepting each other and growing up a bit!"

When I got home after talking with her, there was a message on my answering machine from this same friend. Her voice reflected joy and gratitude: "Sharon, I should have mentioned that one of the reasons I'm doing so much better is that I've been meeting for the past six months with a group of women every week for prayer and Bible study. Oh, how they have prayed for my marriage and me! I know that has made all the difference. In a way, nothing has really changed on the outside, but everything is changed from the inside!"

My favorite book is *Telling Secrets* by Frederick Buechner. He writes eloquently about this vulnerable connection:

> It is important to tell at least from time to time the secret of who
> we truly and fully are—even if we tell it only to ourselves—
> because otherwise we run the risk of losing track of who we truly
> and fully are and little by little come to accept instead the highly
> edited version which we put forth in hope that the world will find
> it more acceptable than the real thing. It is important to tell our
> secrets too because it makes it easier that way to see where we have
> been in our lives and where we are going. It also makes it easier for
> other people to tell us a secret or two of their own, and exchanges
> like that have a lot to do with what being a family is all about.
> Finally, I suspect that it is by entering that deep place inside us
> where our secrets are kept that we come perhaps closer than we
> do anywhere else to the One who, whether we realize it or not, is
> of all our secrets the most telling and the most precious we have
> to tell.[3]

The exercises of discipline, surrender, transparency, and connection are daily, demanding, and delightful practices that will sustain your heart for extravagant love. God's promise to you is filled with images of extravagance: "The LORD will guide you always; he will satisfy your needs in a sun-scorched land and will strengthen your frame. You will be like a well-watered garden, like a spring whose waters never fail" (Isaiah 58:11).

LIVING IN LOVE

For Personal Reflection or Discussion

1. Can you recall a time when you were convicted, determined to live differently, but then became discouraged? What discouraged you?
2. When you think of discipline, what comes to mind?
3. When you think of deliverance, what comes to mind?
4. What do you hope for or in?
5. Do you wish the people in your life were different? How do you think this is noticeable to them and how does it make them feel?

Into Action

1. Create a sacred space for your practice of spiritual disciplines.
2. Pray about a plan for spiritual interactions with friends or family members. Begin courageously following the direction God gives you.
3. Join a small group or consider starting one if a group is not available to you.

CHAPTER 11

A Heart Full of Glory

And we, who with unveiled faces all reflect the Lord's glory,
are being transformed into his likeness
with ever-increasing glory,
which comes from the Lord, who is the Spirit.
(2 Corinthians 3:18)

April 20, 1999, is a day our country will never forget, but it is etched painfully deep in my community—Littleton, Colorado. On April 20, 1999, two high school seniors entered their school, Columbine High School, and shot and bombed their classrooms, library, and cafeteria, wounding many fellow students and killing twelve young men and women and one teacher.

One of my clients had a daughter who was in the high school during the rampage, and she lost a close friend to the shooting. Two months after these tragic events, my client brought her daughter to see me. I will never forget the heartwrenching question this too-old-too-fast seventeen-year-old asked me: "I'm having troubling focusing," she began. "My mind is filled with so many thoughts. I need someone to tell me what is most impor-tant."

I didn't answer her that day. I couldn't. She sat on my couch, waiting halfheartedly for an answer, while we both sobbed. I cried out of my deep sorrow for this young woman who had experienced devastation for which she could not have possibly prepared. And I must tell you, that I also cried for my own newly adolescent daughter and the inevitable heartache she will know in this unpredictable and dangerous world. And yet I found a strange, small comfort in the reality that danger and disappointment often reduce us to the crucial question: *What is most important?* It's the question we started this book with, and the answer is still the same: "Go after a life of love as if your life depended on it—because it does" (1 Corinthians 14:1, *The Message*).

Living for love—extravagant love—is what makes life worth living. Christ calls us to nothing less.

Throughout this book we have examined what keeps us from the life of love and what allows us to love with abandon. I hope the thoughts I've shared with you reflect my own longing to be a woman of extravagant love. But now that I'm writing the final chapter, I find that as with all longing, I want so much more. I want to write it more articulately and describe the life of love more eloquently.

Instead, I will conclude with words from Scripture—with my eventual answer to my client's daughter who asked: *What is most important?* It is the best description of extravagant love written, and I challenge you—daugh-ter, sister, wife, mother, friend—to go after this life of love. Go after it intentionally, daily, fiercely, and prayerfully. You will never regret it, because the challenge to love extravagantly comes with a promise: "Love never fails" (1 Corinthians 13:8)!

The Way of Love

Here is the full text of 1 Corinthians 13—the perfect guide to practicing extravagant love:

If I speak with human eloquence and angelic ecstasy but don't love, I'm nothing but the creaking of a rusty gate.

If I speak God's Word with power, revealing all his mysteries and making everything plain as day, and if I have faith that says to a mountain, "Jump," and it jumps, but I don't love, I'm nothing.

If I give everything I own to the poor and even go to the stake to be burned as a martyr, but I don't love, I've gotten nowhere. So, no matter what I say, what I believe, and what I do, I'm bankrupt without love.

Love never gives up.
Love cares more for others than for self.
Love doesn't want what it doesn't have.
Love doesn't strut,
Doesn't have a swelled head,
Doesn't force itself on others,
Isn't always "me first,"
Doesn't fly off the handle,
Doesn't keep score of the sins of others,
Doesn't revel when others grovel,
Takes pleasure in the flowering of truth,
Puts up with anything,
Trusts God always,

Always looks for the best,
Never looks back,
But keeps going to the end.

Love never dies. Inspired speech will be over some day; praying in tongues will end; understanding will reach its limit. We
know only a portion of the truth, and what we say about God is
always incomplete. But when the Complete arrives, our incom-
pletes will be canceled.

When I was an infant at my mother's breast, I gurgled and
cooed like any infant. When I grew up, I left those infant ways for
good.

We don't yet see things clearly. We're squinting in a fog, peer-
ing through a mist. But it won't be long before the weather clears
and the sun shines bright! We'll see it all then, see it all as clearly as
God sees us, knowing him directly just as he knows us!

But for right now, until that completeness, we have three
things to do to lead us toward that consummation: Trust steadily
in God, hope unswervingly, love extravagantly. And the best of the
three is love. *(The Message)*

Never Give Up

At the beginning of each week, choose a simple, regular activity that you do
without a lot of thought or intention, almost on automatic pilot. You might
choose eating breakfast, waiting in carpool, your coffee break, or daily exercise. Resolve to pause for a minute before you begin this activity and consider
your relationships. Consider using this regular activity to strengthen your
heart for relationships or to awaken you to the possibilities for relationships.

If you choose breakfast time, you might decide to include a prayer time for the needs of your family. You could suggest that everyone pray aloud for someone else in the family. Or you might pray silently for each member of your family and the life of your family as a whole. If you choose your coffee break, you might decide to invite a friend to join you once a week so you can fellowship together.

Often our relationships slide into the mundane or the miserable because we're not paying attention to all the opportunities we have to develop relationships. It's easy to give up when we're tired and bruised by the bumps in the road. But our ability to get up after a night of prayerful anguish on behalf of those we love and make breakfast, pray for our children, or risk again in relationships reveals nobility that surpasses the most regal acts (Proverbs 31:29).

Care More for Others Than for Self

Extravagant love's answer to the question "What is most important?" is "Be kind." Not long ago my husband and I were headed up to bed when he asked: "Sharon, do you think I could have enough of the blanket to cover me tonight?" I don't need to give you all the gory details of the conversation that followed, but suffice it to say that before the evening ended and we actually got into bed, we pulled out a tape measure to measure our bed and blanket to make sure we each had our fair share! By the end of the measuring we were both laughing and aware of how easily and ridiculously simple kindness is extinguished by defensiveness and selfishness.

We have friends who are in the midst of difficulties way beyond our bedroom debate. Pete and Claire have been married for less than a year, and Pete is fighting Hodgkin's disease, a cancer that is waging war against him with all its might. Even though they are in the midst of a lot of pain and fear, both Pete and Claire love to laugh, and so I sheepishly shared with them our story about our bed, our blanket, and the tape measure. I will never forget Claire's response. Gently and without self-righteousness, she simply admitted, "We really don't have that kind of time." None of us do, really. Time is never wasted when we are kind.

Don't Want What You Don't Have

I have a friend who quotes a rather silly song to explain what this means to her. For years she lamented that her husband was not the man of her dreams. She'd hoped that he would become a Sunday school teacher, a leader in the community, and an articulate advocate for their faith. Despite her prayers (and nagging), he remained painfully shy, an introvert, and often at a loss for words in the midst of a group of people.

She explains that God "hit her over the head" with a song playing over the loudspeaker at Kmart. The singer crooned, "If you can't be with the one you love, love the one you're with." She believes God used the intercom at Kmart to remind her that a life of love is not about waiting for others to become the people we can love, but about loving the people we're already with. I agree. And in loving, we discover love.

Don't Strut

When your relationships flourish, don't get cocky. Instead, be grateful. Gratitude keeps us in a posture to continue receiving.

At the end of each day, take a few moments to recall all the pleasant experiences and also take note of those that were uncomfortable or disappointing. Give thanks for all the people who touched your life today. Name any gratitude you feel for each person. Next, recall the painful encounters. Try to give thanks for those encounters as well, expressing gratitude for what the event might have taught you, what it helped you notice about yourself.

What do you experience as you practice giving thanks for something

painful? Are you softer or angrier? At the end of a week of practicing gratitude, what do you notice about how you perceive your life? We tend to
misunderstand the link between joy and gratefulness. We observe that joy-
ful people are grateful and suppose they are grateful for their joy. The oppo-
site is true: Joy springs from gratitude.

Don't Have a Swelled Head

Two friends and I recently attended a professional seminar addressing, in
part, strategies for counseling men and women differently based on gender
distinctions. The speaker used film clips to illustrate some of his points.
When he highlighted male characteristics he used a scene from the movie
Braveheart. Our hearts swelled with the passion of the scene in which the
courageous Scottish warrior William Wallace, face painted and spear in
hand, mounted his horse, whooped with cries for freedom, and led his men
into valiant battle. What a picture of bravery!

When the speaker began to address female characteristics, he showed a
scene from the movie *Little Women.* The scene showed Marmee reading to
her children. The women in the audience moaned a collective, "Ugh."
Marmee seemed bland compared to Braveheart Wallace!

My friends and I talked about the different film clips during our lunch
break and brainstormed about the scenes we might use to illustrate the
strengths and unique qualities of a woman. We felt a little disheartened at
first, because it seemed that every example we came up with fell far short of
the passionate battle scene in *Braveheart.* We discovered that all of our
examples were scenes of women in the midst of stories about relationships.
These stories don't, on their face, look like exciting tales of adventure and
bravery. But a humble heart is sustained and strengthened as we realize that
unrecognized acts of virtue are just that—acts of virtue.

I remember something novelist Barbara Kingsolver wrote:

For women, like me, it seems, it's not ours to take charge of begin-
nings and endings. Not the marriage proposal, the summit con-
quered, the first shot fired, nor the last one either—the treaty at
Appomattox, the knife in the heart. Let men write those stories. I
can't. I only know the middle ground where we live our lives. We
whistle while Rome burns, or we scrub the floor, depending. Don't
presume there's shame in the lot of a woman who carries on. *Con-
quest* and *liberation*…are words that mean squat, basically, when
you have hungry children and clothes out on the line and it looks
like rain.[1]

Not having a swelled head allows us to recognize that reading to our
children, encouraging a disheartened friend, making valentines for our husband, and folding the laundry are acts of significant value. Some women
may lead companies into the Fortune 500, travel to space, or find a cure for
a dreaded disease—and we will cheer them on. But finding honor in the
daily tasks of relationships is an adventure of heroic proportions that is
strengthened by humility, not war paint and weaponry.

Don't Force Yourself on Others

When relationships are tense, disappointing, or mundane, our heart full of
longing for the people we love can tempt us to swoop down on them with
an intensity that can be destructive. Sometimes after a hard day of work,
my husband doesn't really want to go into the details of his day. When I ask
how the day went, he might reply, "Fine." Because I sense his fatigue and
tension, I know the day was anything but "fine." I want to know more. I

want conversation. I want details, and quite frankly, I want him to ask about my day. I become like a yippy terrier that follows my husband around, nipping at his heels, whimpering and even barking for attention.

I am learning that not forcing myself on others requires patience, sensitivity, and the grace to wait winsomely. For me, this means honestly expressing: "I'd love to know more about your day when you feel like talking. In the meantime, can I bring you a glass of iced tea?" Waiting winsomely is part of the invigorating work of extravagant love. When relationships do not go as quickly or smoothly as we'd like, can we remain kind, inviting, and expectant?

Not forcing ourselves on others means that in the midst of waiting we hold on to the ending we prayerfully envision for those we love, while allowing the waiting to transform us into kinder, more patient, more creative, more grace-filled women.

Don't Concentrate Always on "Me First"

A "me first" agenda makes it more important for my son to take out the trash than for him to learn the rewards of hard work. This agenda manipulates my husband into attending the small group I want to be in rather than learning more about his fear of talking in groups and discovering together what would be a comfortable setting for us both. My agenda lists what I want my friend to know about me without considering what might be going on in her life. A "me first" agenda is work-oriented, short-sighted, self-satisfying, and often directly opposes living with faith, hope, and love.

Don't Fly off the Handle

The work of extravagant love involves asking myself, before I respond in difficult relationships, *Who do I want to be?* A life of love is possible to the degree I determine to reflect God's image rather than my reaction to the disappointing behaviors of the people I love.

When my husband is grumpy, who do I want to be? If I become angry, distant, or demanding, I am reflecting his behavior. If I am patient, kind, and empathetic, I am reflecting the image of God and using my husband's bad day to transform me further into the image of Christ. When my friend neglects me and doesn't call for weeks and I respond with a determination that she'll never hear from me again, I am reflecting her hurtful behavior. When I call her and initiate getting together with warmth and curiosity about where she's been, I am reflecting Christ's heart of open invitation.

No relationship is perfect; we ourselves are not perfect. Every relationship is filled with opportunities to polish off parts of ourselves, "being transformed into his likeness with ever-increasing glory" (2 Corinthians 3:18).

Don't Keep Score of the Sins of Others

Always be open to forgiveness, waiting and ready to be reconciled to one who has hurt or disappointed you. Being open to forgiveness does not mean that you allow someone to sin against you repeatedly or sweep wrongdoings under the carpet. Being open to forgiveness means that we no longer hold on to how someone hurt or dishonored us. We allow God to bring that person to repentance, and in the meantime we are free to go our own way and continue in the life of love. Keeping score of the sins of another traps us in a never-ending dance of resentment with that person.

Don't Revel When Others Grovel

Extravagant love is rich with compassion, knowing that we all suffer from the same condition: We all "fall short of the glory of God" (Romans 3:23).

Others' failure becomes an opportunity for us to demonstrate most power-fully the love of Christ, who "while we were still sinners…died for us" (Romans 5:8).

Failure also is an opportunity for relationships to be deepened, trust to be solidified, and hearts to be united. The Spanish philosopher Miguel de Unamuno says it most eloquently in *Tragic Sense of Life:* "Great love is born of sorrow. It is then that we know one another and feel one another and feel with one another in common anguish, and so thus we pity one another and love one another. For to love is to pity; and if bodies are united by pleasure, souls are united by pain…. To love with the spirit is to pity, and [she] who pities most loves most."

Take Pleasure in the Flowering of Truth

In the Greek language there are two words for time. The first is *chronos* and describes chronological time, the measure of minutes, hours, days, months, and years. The second is *kairos*, which is translated in the Bible as "the full-ness of time." This sense of time describes the blossoming of something when it is ready to flower.

We long for relationships to be born, nurtured, and mature—today. Waiting for the flowering of truth—a friend to develop spiritually, a hus-band to understand our longings, a son or daughter to develop maturity, or ourselves to grow spiritually—is often the crucible of transformation for us. To take pleasure in this waiting compels us to wait on God and to note the fruits of waiting.

Tamara is one of my heroes in the life of love. She leads a ministry for teens who live on the streets of inner-city Denver. When I first met her, she often expressed to me her longing to be a wife and mother and her impa-tience in waiting for the seeds of this longing to bear fruit. Last year, through Tamara's work, she met a seven-year-old girl named Grace. When Tamara first met her, Grace had not been to school in months because she stayed home to care for her younger brothers and sisters.

Through the proper authorities, Tamara got permission to bring Grace to her home in a foster-care arrangement. Tamara's first task was to rid Grace of lice and to find shoes for the barefoot girl. Tamara has cared for Grace for over a year and is watching her flower into a happy, healthy little girl.

When I met Tamara for lunch recently, she told me what she has learned about waiting. "I used to sit at home waiting for God to bring love into my life, and I thought I knew what it would look like. I was growing into a bitter woman. I have learned that waiting is active and that, in loving the seven-year-old God brought into my life, I am the woman I always wanted to be and my life is overflowing with love!"

The flowering of truth in Tamara's life "give[s] off a sweet scent rising to God, which is recognized by those on the way of salvation—an aroma redolent with life" (2 Corinthians 2:16, *The Message*).

Put Up with Anything

Forbearance, the characteristic described here, is to endure, to exercise patience and restraint. Forbearance does not mean that we conceal the truth or are dishonest about the realities of our lives. Forbearance does not mean we let people walk all over us. Forbearance describes another posture of the heart: The life of love requires a spiritual practice that waits. We are compelled to discover what is reliable and true as we listen to our hearts and listen to the "still, small voice" of the Spirit that leads us in the path of love.

In her book *When the Heart Waits*, Sue Monk Kidd describes the practice of forbearance:

I had tended to view waiting as mere passivity. When I looked it up in my dictionary however, I found that the words *passive* and *passion* come from the same Latin root, *pati*, which means "to endure." Waiting is thus both passive and passionate. It's a vibrant, contemplative work. It means descending into self, into God, into the deeper labyrinths of prayer. It involves listening to disinherited voices within, facing the wounded holes in the soul, the denied and undiscovered, the places one lives falsely. It means struggling with the vision of who we really are in God and molding the courage to live that vision.[2]

Trust God Always

The spiritual practice of guarding our hearts for the life of love always leads us to intimate conversations with God that increase our knowledge of him and deepen our faith.

One of my daughter's dear friends is a fellow eighth-grader named Erin. Erin and Kristin have experienced together the roller coaster relationships of middle school and often share their hurts and hopes about friendship. Last year, Erin felt outcast from the popular girls at school and began to write poetry to express her jumble of emotions. Here are a few lines from one of her poems:

> I see their happy faces,
> The girls excluding me.
> I see the hurt in others' eyes
> Going through the same as me.

Her adolescent angst, which we all can recall as a familiar part of growing up, has given way to an extraordinary faith. Over the summer, Erin organized a Bible study with fellow students to study topics like gossip, friendship, dating, and kindness. Only a few girls attended, but they developed some close friendships.

Once school started, Erin suggested to her friends that they try a unique fast one week every quarter. They would eat their regular breakfast and dinner, but for lunch they would eat one fruit that they would associate with a fruit of the Spirit. They would meditate on that "fruit" throughout their school day, hoping that their hearts would not be overtaken by the anger, jealousy, and depression that teenage relationships often produce.

Just yesterday Erin said to Kristin, "I'm kind of glad I'm not part of the 'popular group.' As a result, I have such a big relationship with God!" In Erin's eighth-grade faith, we see the shape of extravagant love.

Always Look for the Best

When we practice seeing with our hearts, we discover that we do not need different people or circumstances to look at, we just need to look at the people and circumstances in our lives differently!

Not too long ago my mother introduced me to a woman who exemplifies this characteristic of extravagant love. I met Evelyn near the end of her recovery from a broken hip. Her husband had recently suffered a debilitating stroke and was in a nursing home. I asked her, "Did marriage turn out like you expected it to? And aren't you disappointed that it's ended with deteriorating health for both of you?"

She smiled when she answered, "I am looking for new ways to let my husband know how much I love him." She told me about a recent project in which she took a picture of their family, grandkids and pets included, and had it enlarged to life-size and set it in his room. Tears streamed down his face, she said, as they looked together at the picture and gave thanks for their family.

Looking for the best requires seeing the landscape of our lives with gratitude, which further sharpens our ability to see through the lens of the heart.

Never Look Back

I don't believe the apostle Paul's words in 1 Corinthians are intended to encourage us to forget our past, but rather to live without regret. But how do we live, never looking back?

The Russian poet Anna Akhmatova wrote, "I warn you, I am living here on earth for the last time." Determine, like Anna, to live while you are alive! Do you need to say: "I love you," "I'd like to help," or "Let's start over"? Is there one small step you could take today to restore a relationship, revive your passion for a dream, or deepen your relationship with God?

Keep Going to the End

The description of extravagant love ends as it begins: *Never give up. Keep going.*

An anonymous poet describes the cycle of the life of love:

Thou has made me endless,
Such is thy pleasure.
This frail vessel thou emptiest
Again and again, and fillest
It ever with fresh life.
Ages pass and still thou pourest,
And still there is room to fill.

Living with the anticipation of not only what could be but also what *will* be is what allows us to hang on:

Then he told me, "These are those who come from the great tribulation, and they've washed their robes, scrubbed them clean in the blood of the Lamb. That's why they're standing before God's Throne. They serve him day and night in his Temple. The One on the Throne will pitch his tent there for them: no more hunger, no more thirst, no more scorching heat. The Lamb on the Throne will shepherd them, will lead them to spring waters of Life. And God will wipe every last tear from their eyes." (Revelation 7:14-17, *The Message*)

THE WONDER OF HIS LOVE

As you have read through this book and reflected on your own longings, I suspect at different times your heart has leapt within you as you've contemplated the people and the circumstances of your life, and maybe you've whispered, "Oh, I want to be an extravagant lover." But then the telephone rings, your husband hurts your feelings, your children complain about dinner, or a friend forgets your birthday.

How can we be extraordinary lovers—daughters, sisters, wives, mothers, friends—in an ordinary, sinful world?

The apostle John offers the answer: "God is love. When we take up permanent residence in a life of love, we live in God and God lives in us. This way, love has the run of the house, becomes at home and mature in us.... [We] are going to love—love and be loved. First we were loved, now we love. He loved us first.... We know it so well, we've embraced it heart and soul, this love that comes from God" (1 John 4:16-17,19,16, *The Message*).

Embrace this truth with your heart and soul. He loved us *first.* Scripture reveals that Jesus lived out the traits listed in 1 Corinthians 13. His love provides the model for us to imitate.

He Never Gives Up

"With God on our side like this, how can we lose?…The One who died for us—who was raised to life for us!—is in the presence of God at this very moment sticking up for us. Do you think anyone is going to be able to drive a wedge between us and Christ's love for us? There is no way! Not trouble, not hard times, not hatred, not hunger, not homelessness, not bullying threats, not backstabbing, not even the worst sins listed in Scripture…. Nothing living or dead, angelic or demonic, today or tomorrow, high or low, thinkable or unthinkable—absolutely *nothing* can get between us and God's love because of the way that Jesus our Master has embraced us" (Romans 8:31-39, *The Message*).

He Cares More for Others Than for Self

"In kindness, he takes us firmly by the hand and leads us into a radical life change" (Romans 2:4, *The Message*).

He Doesn't Want What He Doesn't Have

"He didn't, and doesn't, wait for us to get ready. He presented himself for this sacrificial death when we were far too weak and rebellious to do anything to get ourselves ready. And even if we hadn't been so weak, we wouldn't have known what to do anyway. We can understand someone dying for a person worth dying for, and we can understand how someone good and noble could inspire us to selfless sacrifice. But God put his love on the line for us by offering his Son in sacrificial death while we were of no use whatever to him" (Romans 5:6-8, *The Message*).

He Doesn't Strut

"Think of yourselves the way Christ Jesus thought of himself. He had equal status with God but didn't think so much of himself that he had to cling to the advantages of that status no matter what. Not at all. When the time came, he set aside the privileges of deity and took on the status of a slave, became *human!* Having become human, he stayed human.... He didn't claim special privileges. Instead, he lived a selfless, obedient life and then died a selfless, obedient death—and the worst kind of death at that: a crucifixion" (Philippians 2:5-8, *The Message*).

He Doesn't Have a Swelled Head

"Just before the Passover Feast, Jesus knew that the time had come to leave this world to go to the Father. Having loved his dear companions, he continued to love them right to the end. It was suppertime.... Jesus knew that the Father had put him in complete charge of everything, that he came from God and was on his way back to God. So he got up from the supper table, set aside his robe, and put on an apron. Then he poured water into a basin and began to wash the feet of the disciples, drying them with his apron" (John 13:1-5, *The Message*).

He Doesn't Act As If It's Always "Me First"

"Look at me. I stand at the door. I knock. If you hear me call and open the door, I'll come right in and sit down to supper with you" (Revelation 3:20, *The Message*).

He Doesn't Fly off the Handle

"He was oppressed and afflicted, yet he did not open his mouth; he was led like a lamb to the slaughter, and as a sheep before her shearers is silent, so he did not open his mouth" (Isaiah 53:7).

He Doesn't Keep Score of Our Sins

"Because of the sacrifice of the Messiah, his blood poured out on the altar of the Cross, we're a free people—free of penalties and punishments chalked up by all our misdeeds. And not just barely free, either. *Abundantly free!*" (Ephesians 1:7, *The Message*).

He Doesn't Revel When We Grovel

"Since we've compiled this long and sorry record as sinners…and proved that we are utterly incapable of living the glorious lives God wills for us, God did it for us. Out of sheer generosity he put us in right standing with himself. A pure gift" (Romans 3:23-25, *The Message*).

He Puts Up with Anything

He is forbearing. "Keep your eyes on Jesus, who both began and finished this race we're in. Study how he did it. Because he never lost sight of where he was headed—that exhilarating finish in and with God—he could put up with anything along the way: cross, shame, whatever. And now he's *there*, in the place of honor, right alongside God. When you find yourselves flagging in your faith, go over that story again, item by item, that long litany of hostility he plowed through. *That* will shoot adrenaline into your souls!" (Hebrews 12:2, *The Message*).

He Trusts His Father Always

"I glorified you on earth by completing down to the last detail what you assigned me to do…. I spelled out your character in detail to the men and women you gave me. They know now…that everything you gave me is firsthand from you…. Righteous Father, the world has never known you, but I have known you, and these disciples know that you sent me on this mission. I have made your very being known to them—who you are and what you do—and continue to make it known, so that your love for me might be in them" (John 17:4,6,25-26, *The Message*).

He Always Looks for the Best

Christ's love for the church is "marked by giving, not getting. Christ's love makes the church whole. His words evoke her beauty. Everything he does and says is designed to bring the best out of her, dressing her in dazzling white silk, radiant with holiness" (Ephesians 5:25-27, *The Message*).

He Never Looks Back

"Again he prayed, 'My Father, if there is no other way than this, drinking this cup to the dregs, I'm ready. Do it your way'" (Matthew 26:42, *The Message*). "He concludes, 'I'll forever wipe the slate clean of their sins.' Once sins are taken care of for good, there's no longer any need to offer sacrifices for them" (Hebrews 10:17-18, *The Message*).

He Keeps Going to the End

"Don't let [trials] throw you. You trust God, don't you? Trust me. There is plenty of room for you in my Father's home. If that weren't so, would I have told you that I'm on my way to get a room ready for you? And if I'm on my way to get your room ready, I'll come back and get you so you can live where I live" (John 14:1-3, *The Message*).

"I'll never let you down, never walk off and leave you" (Hebrews 13:5, *The Message*).

As we look "unto Jesus, the author and finisher of our faith" (Hebrews 12:2, KJV), we "suddenly recognize that God is a living, personal presence, not a piece of chiseled stone. And when God is personally present, a living Spirit, that old, constricting legislation is recognized as obsolete. We're free of it! All of us! Nothing between us and God, our faces shining with the brightness of his face.... Our lives gradually becoming brighter and more beautiful as God enters our lives and we become like him" (2 Corinthians 3:17-18, *The Message*).

Dear woman—daughter, sister, wife, mother, friend—*go after the life of love as if your life depended on it, because it does.* And in so doing you will discover the love of your life.

O Deus, ego amo te

O God, I love thee, I love thee—
Not out of hope of heaven for me
Nor fearing not to love and be
In the everlasting burning.
Thou, thou, my Jesus, after me
Didst reach thine arms out dying,
For my sake sufferedst nails and lance,
Mocked and marred countenance,
Sorrows passing number,
Sweat and care and cumber,
Yea and death, and this for me,
And thou couldst see me sinning:
Then I, why should not I love thee,
Jesus, so much in love with me?
Not for heaven's sake; not to be
Out of hell by loving thee;
Not for any gains I see;
But just the way that thou didst me

I do love and I will love thee;
What must I love for then?
For being my king and God. Amen.

—Gerard Manley Hopkins (1844-1889)

Notes

Chapter 2: A Holy Desire

1. Frank E. Gaebelein, ed., *The Expositor's Bible Commentary*, vol. 2 (Grand Rapids, Mich.: Zondervan, 1990), 57.

2. Peter G. Van Breemen, *Certain As the Dawn* (Denville, N.J.: Dimension Books, 1980), 13.

Chapter 3: Loving from a Whole Heart

1. Paul Pearsall, Ph.D., *The Heart's Code* (New York: Broadway Books, 1998), 27.

2. Frederick Buechner, *Now and Then* (San Francisco: Harper & Row, 1983), 15-6.

Chapter 4: The Queen of Hearts

1. Anne Lamott, *Traveling Mercies* (New York: Pantheon Books, 1999), 20.

2. Oswald Chambers, *My Utmost for His Highest* (Grand Rapids, Mich.: Discovery House, 1992), May 9 devotion.

Chapter 7: Bravehearts

1. Rachel Naomi Remen, *Kitchen Table Wisdom* (New York: Riverhead, 1996), 35.

2. Jack Hayford, *A New Time and Place* (Sisters, Oreg.: Multnomah Books, 1997), 97.

Chapter 8: A Redeemed Heart

1. As quoted by Dan Wakefield, *The Story of Your Life* (Boston: Beacon Press, 1990), 95-6.

2. Dominic Maruca, "A Reflection on Guilt," *Human Development* 3:1 (spring 1982): 42.

3. Jan O. Rowe et al., "The Psychology of Forgiving Another: A Dialogal Research Approach," in *Existential-Phenomenological Perspectives in Psychology: Exploring the Breadth of Human Experience,* ed. Ronald S. Valle and Steen Halling (New York: Plenum, 1989), 233-44.

Chapter 9: Heart Skills

1. Hayford, *Time and Place,* 28.

2. Brennan Manning, *A Stranger to Self-Hatred* (Denville, N.J.: Dimension Books, 1982), 123.

3. Dean Ornish, M.D., *Love and Survival: Eight Pathways to Intimacy and Health* (New York: HarperCollins, 1998), 29.

Chapter 10: Sustaining Your Heart

1. Dallas Willard, *The Spirit of the Disciplines* (San Francisco: Harper & Row, 1988), xii.

2. Elizabeth Berg, *The Pull of the Moon* (New York: Jove, 1997), 49.

3. Frederick Buechner, *Telling Secrets* (New York: HarperCollins, 1992), 3.

Chapter 11: A Heart Full of Glory

1. Barbara Kingsolver, *The Poisonwood Bible* (New York: HarperCollins, 1998), 383.

2. Sue Monk Kidd, *When the Heart Waits* (New York: HarperCollins, 1991), 14.

About the Author

Sharon A. Hersh is a daughter, sister, wife, mom, and friend. She is also a licensed professional counselor specializing in relational issues, who has worked with hundreds of women in her private practice. She is the director of Women's Recovery & Renewal, a ministry of counseling, retreat, and support services for struggling women and their caregivers.

Sharon's articles have been published in *The Mars Hill Review* and *Today's Christian Woman*. She is a frequent speaker at conferences and retreats, and she and her husband speak for Family Life, a worldwide ministry of Campus Crusade for Christ, which hosts conferences on marriage and parenting. Sharon lives in Littleton, Colorado, with her husband and two children.